ADVANCE PRAISE FOR MIRIAM MULÉY'S

The 85% Niche: The Power of Women of All Colors—Latina, Black, Asian

"*The 85% Niche: The Power of Women of All Colors* integrates classical brand management principles with diversity and gender marketing expertise. It reflects Miriam's years of experience and knowledge on marketing to women and marketing to multicultural women. Kudos to Miriam for using smarts, savvy, and creative thinking to push the envelope on the subject of marketing to women."

C. J. FRALEIGH   *CEO, Sara Lee Beverage & Foods*

"As a business woman who has successfully developed marketing plans for several brands at large, medium and small companies, Miriam understands how to sell to women and to multicultural consumers. *The 85% Niche: The Power of Women of All Colors* represents a concise professional view of what drives women of *diverse* backgrounds to consider a brand for future purchase. Muléy understands the strategic, operational and diversity aspects of marketing. This is a highly recommend read for today's global companies."

MICHAEL JACKSON   *CMO, Summa Entertainment*
Former Vice President & General Manager, Vehicle Sales, Service & Marketing, General Motors Corporation

"The 85% Niche actually creates a dialogue with a variety of women at different levels to understand these micro cultures. It is a wonderful and unique concept because it creates an ongoing exchange with women from all stations and from all cultures so that they then can help companies understand what's next, what their needs are, what's evolving in the marketplace. It's real time and it's useful information that the companies can rely on to plan and to be successful in the marketplace."

GILLIAN HORSHAM   *Product Director, American Greeting Cards*

"*The 85% Niche: The Power of Women of All Colors* is an expertly written book on diversity marketing with a specific specialty in strategy formulation and implementation of marketing efforts targeted to women. Ms. Muléy's passion for enhancing market penetration for the diverse consumer is keenly noted throughout these pages. Her work is focused, professional, and knowledgeable. She is an authority on diversity and the value it brings to enhanced performance results in a highly competitive marketplace."

VICTORIA E. JONES *HR Director and Dean*
College of Leadership, General Motors Corporation, Retired

"I am delighted to wholeheartedly endorse Miriam Muléy and her book, *The 85% Niche: The Power of Women of All Colors.* She brings fresh perspective to the opportunity so many companies, especially direct selling companies, have in marketing and selling to women of color. Read this book, and then read it again for the wonderful insights it offers."

NICKI KEOHOHOU *President, Direct Selling Women's Alliance*

"The principals of *The 85% Niche: The Power of Women of All Colors*—recognizing the power of women of diverse ethnic, cultural and socioeconomic backgrounds in developing advertising and marketing plans—is long over due. Miriam Muléy's foresight and leadership in bringing this book to the Boardrooms of Corporate America, her personal experiences as a Latina woman of color and her professional credentials as a businesswoman uniquely position her to deliver exceptional results and business solutions in marketing to *all* women. Period."

BYRON E. LEWIS *Chairman, UniWorld Group, Inc.*

"The African Methodist Episcopal Church (AME) has long recognized the power of African American women in the Black Church. It's refreshing to read *The 85% Niche: The Power of Women of All Colors* and see that corporations are finally getting it and know what we have known for years: Black women are a much to be respected community of leaders."

BISHOP E. EARL MCCLOUD, JR.
Member, Council of Bishops African Methodist Episcopal Church

"I highly recommend this book to any company interested in increasing market share among consumers and among women in particular. Miriam's past strong track record of success in managing diversity for bottom line results, her deep knowledge on all aspects of diversity management—from advertising, publicity, promotions, product development, supplier engagements, sales strategies, and leveraging the power of corporate philanthropy—are intricately woven throughout this book. She has a bias for action and it shows in this book."

VIVIAN PICKARD *Director, Corporate Relations, General Motors Corp. President Black Women's Agenda; Chair-Elect, Inforum*

"Miriam's book, *The 85% Niche: The Power of Women of All Colors,* is a highly credible analysis of what it takes to grow market share among consumers in general, and among diverse consumers, in particular. As former General Director for the Women's Retail Initiative at General Motors, and given the increasingly important role that women play in fueling the economic engine of the automotive industry, I believe Miriam's work, experiences and insights on how to create and implement an integrated diversity business plan will be of tremendous value and learning to readers of this book."

PATRICIA J. ROBERTS *Former General Director, Women's Retail Initiative, General Motors Corporation*

"*The 85% Niche: The Power of Women of All Colors* is a powerful and thought-provoking business book. It addresses the subject of marketing to women and marketing to women of color in a unique and refreshing way. As a businesswoman, as a woman of Puerto Rican ancestry, and as a woman of color, Miriam uses her knowledge and experience to successfully "peel back the layers" around marketing to women and uncovers important differences from a cultural and ethnic point of view. Read this book to understand how you can sharpen your knowledge around what really drives women and women of color."

JOYCE M. ROCHÉ *President & CEO, Girls, Inc.*

"Finally, someone has stepped forward with the leadership, vision, and business knowledge to shed light on the diversity that exists among women. Miriam's approach to lifestyle and diversity segmentation fills a huge gap in the marketplace. She's hit the nail on the head with great clarity about the impact of life stage on gender, culture and ethnicity. And, she brings clarity to the wide range of diversity that exists among women of African descent—Afro Puerto Rican women, Afro Cuban women, Caribbean women and more—we all share a common history."

DR. MARTA VEGA *Founder & CEO, The Caribbean Cultural Center*

Practical Books for Smart Marketers from PMP

Now you can equip all your sales people with **The 85% Niche: The Power of Women of All Colors.** It will help them introduce new solutions to your existing customers and open the doors for new business development. You may also want to distribute the book to potential customers to help them understand the size and purchasing power of this market and its implications for their industry.

A customized edition, with *"Compliments of* **Your Company Name***"* on the cover is available with orders of 200 or more copies.

Call us toll-free at **888-787-8100** for quotes on quantity orders.

For more practical books for smart marketers, go to our website, **www.paramountbooks.com**.

The 85% Niche

The Power of Women of All Colors —
Latina, Black, Asian

MIRIAM MULÉY

PMP

Paramount Market Publishing, Inc.

8/25/09
WW
$ 39.95

Paramount Market Publishing, Inc.
950 Danby Road, Suite 136
Ithaca, NY 14850
www.paramountbooks.com
Telephone: 607-275-8100; 888-787-8100   Facsimile: 607-275-8101

Publisher: James Madden
Editorial Director: Doris Walsh

Cover photo: A. Perry Heller Photography

Cataloging in Publication Data available
ISBN 13: 978-0-9801745-5-7 | ISBN 10: 0-9801745-5-4

I DEDICATE THIS BOOK to my mother, Margarita Cecilia Rosa Muléy who taught me how to make an incredible *arroz con gandules* and who showed me how to be a true *mujer Latina*: dedicated to family, loving without limits, and passionate for all of the good that Life has to offer.

I ALSO DEDICATE THIS BOOK to my father, Ramón "Moncho" Muléy, my first hero, whose sacrifice to buy a desk and typewriter for his then twelve-year-old daughter sparked her journey as a writer.

Thank you both for being my first role models.

Ustedes me han dado la fuerza, el apoyo y el deseo de siempre
salir adelante en la vida—en la "lucha interminable."
Les quiero mucho y dedico este libro a sus sueños y a su amor.
Siempre vivirán en mi corazón y ahora en éstas páginas.

Contents

Foreword

AT GENERAL MOTORS CORPORATION, our mission is to create a culture and a business environment based upon inclusion, mutual respect, responsibility, and understanding. We value the broad constituency of consumers, regardless of gender, race, ethnicity, culture, religion, veteran status, age, and sexual orientation, who represent the landscape of the new America. Diversity is no longer just a statistic that we read in business books or an ethnic group that lives in a state far removed from where we live or do business. Diversity is truly the America of *today*. And, with more than 60 percent of all new car, truck, and crossover purchases made by women, Hispanics, African-Americans, Asians, youth, and the gay and lesbian markets, we at General Motors understand the importance of diversity to our bottom line. We utilize a diverse workforce to design, build, and sell "gotta have" world-class, environmentally friendly, and fuel-efficient vehicles. We also work with a diverse team of subject matter experts to infuse cultural sensitivity throughout General Motors, helping us to better understand these powerful and diverse consumer groups.

Miriam Muléy well understands the importance of diversity to a company's bottom line. In her role as Executive Director of Diversity Marketing and Sales Strategy, she was pivotal in rallying the forces within GM to focus marketing and sales to reach and sell to women and to the growing, diverse, and increasingly affluent new vehicle buyers—Hispanics, African Americans, Asians, youth, and the gay and lesbian markets.

Her book, *The 85% Niche: The Power of Women of All Colors* offers business leaders the opportunity to connect with women on a cultural and ethnic level. Miriam takes the discussion of marketing to women to a new level by delving more deeply into the "who" of the women's market. Rather than taking a monolithic view of women, Miriam provides practical insight into what it means to be a Latina woman, a Black woman, and an Asian woman. She effectively translates these insights into compelling marketing best practices that business leaders can quickly integrate into planning efforts.

Why you should read this book

Surprisingly, despite the growing importance of diversity in America and the economic vibrancy of the women's market, there is a need for more credible, fact-based marketing intelligence on the subject of gender/diversity marketing. *The 85% Niche: The Power of Women of All Colors* closes this knowledge gap. It guides the reader through a comprehensive, step-by-step learning process, outlining in great detail the economic buying power represented by women of color and the business case supporting the need to target this audience for maximum and sustained business results.

Miriam demonstrates the "hidden" power of women as a dominant buying group, influencing upwards of 85% of all product and service purchase decisions. She also characterizes the complexity of what lies "below the surface" of female buyers from a diversity point of view and discusses how this complexity warrants changes in marketing messages, product design, promotional programs, sales training, philanthropy, and customer service. The unique size, shape, and dimensions of the women's market are inherent in their language, food, music, art, spiritual expression, physical appearance, lifestyle, and traditions. Finally, Miriam successfully demonstrates that women have "broken away" from the mainstream and seek greater levels of independence, self-esteem and economic empowerment. *The 85% Niche: The Power of Women of All Colors* shows how the growth in women's earning and spending power, coupled with their increasing decision-making autonomy, makes them *the* essential target audience for every company that hopes to succeed in today's marketplace.

Miriam's goals in writing this book are to be applauded. While many companies, advertising agencies, and authors have initiated dialog on marketing to women, Miriam sees this as just the beginning. For her, the landscape of the women's market has fundamentally changed and is far more sophisticated than many would suggest. She has created a matrix or, as we like to say at GM, a "basket-weave" approach to thinking about bridges that connect *gender* insights with *diversity* insights. And she infuses *life stage* with gender and diversity insights to create a truly powerful message for readers. She uncovers critical marketing intelligence that can help companies create more effective business strategies by leveraging the power of *all* women.

I am not aware of any other author who has approached the subject of marketing to women in the manner that Miriam does. Her approach is to "think globally" in relation to building brand consideration for women, but to "act locally" in tactical efforts that appeal to the different needs of Latina women, African-American women, Asian women and other key ethnic groups in this country. That's just good business sense.

GARY L. COWGER
Group Vice President, General Motors Corporation

Acknowledgements

As a first-time author, I have many individuals to thank in the creation of this book. First and foremost, I wish to thank my family and close friends for believing in me and giving me greater confidence as I journeyed in the writing of this book. Were it not for them, I'm not sure where I would be. Thank you Tití Awilda, Elba, Haydeé, Margie, Abdul, Nydia, and Pat for being my biggest fan club.

There are many, many business leaders, colleagues, and associates to whom I will be forever grateful. Gary Cowger, Group Vice-President at General Motors Corporation, has left an indelible mark as a senior leader and champion for diversity. His leadership, vision, and tough standards for diversity as a business imperative paved the way for several major and groundbreaking initiatives at the company. Rod Gillum, Vice President of Diversity and Corporate Relations at General Motors is steadfast in his commitment to diversity and inclusion. Thank you for being among those trusted executives who encouraged me to write this book.

Joyce Roché, President of Girls, Inc., and Harriet Edelman, former Chief Information Officer for Avon Products, Inc., thank you for being my first true businesswomen role models and for showing me that women *can* have it all! Fredia Roberson, Senior Vice President and Management Supervisor at Campbell-Ewald, Colleen Robar, Director of Communications at Crain Publications, Vivian Pickard, Director of Corporate Relations at GM, and Patricia Russell-McCloud—one of the finest motivational speakers on this planet and former President of The Links, Inc., I am forever in debt for your support and prayers. Your belief in me has not waned.

To Dr. Marta Vega, founder of The Caribbean Cultural Center, to Dr. José Méndez-Andino, to Josy Laza Gallagher, co-founder of Madrinas—a national not-for-profit (501(c)3) organization dedicated to supporting the career advancement of Latinas in today's corporate/ business environment and Senior Consultant at FutureWorks Institute, we are on a journey to "make the invisible, visible" and to elevate awareness of the diversity within the Hispanic communities.

To Delia Passi, a true visionary and expert in selling to women, thank you for your relentless pursuit of excellence. I owe a tremendous debt to Marti Barletta, expert in marketing to women, and to Anne Doyle, CEO of Anne Doyle Strategies and named one of the "100 Leading Women in the North American Automotive Industry." You cheered me on from the start with resources, contacts, and suggestions on how to move my book proposal forward. To Mary Lou Quinlan, a mentor, friend, and colleague, I say "thank you" for your energy, zeal, and role-modeling. Now I know why our paths crossed over 20 years ago at Avon Products, Inc.! And last, but certainly not least, to Herb Kemp, trusted advisor, former-boss, and true friend . . . I have tremendous admiration and respect for you.

No book concept is realized without the strength and "know how" of a publishing team. To this I am grateful to Doris Walsh, editorial director of Paramount Market Publishing and to Sarah Dickman, my agent. Your comments and recommendations have resulted in a powerful product.

Finally, I want to thank my family. Thank you to my husband, Elket and to our children, Elket Jr., Jasmine, Khayyam, and Destinee for being a constant source of inspiration. I could not have done this without you.

Disclaimer

EXCEPT WHERE AFFILIATED with obviously identified corporations or organizations, names and identities used throughout the book have been changed.

Although the term *women of color* has been used by others predominantly in relation to African-American women, I intend a much broader definition of its use in this book. The term, *women of color,* refers to women of many distinct ethnic, racial, and cultural groups including women of Hispanic, African, Asian, and Native American descent. It also extends beyond age to include all females of color, i.e., those who are under age 21 and those who are adults, including senior citizens.

The terms African American, Black, persons of African descent, the African Diaspora, Afro Caribbean and Afro Latino ancestry are used to direct focus to persons whose racial origin traces to Africa. African American and Black are used interchangeably, although it is acknowledged that roughly half of the U.S. African descended population prefers the use of *African American,* while the other half prefers the use of *Black.*

English grammar standards indicate the use of lower case punctuation when speaking of race, as in the case of "black" or "white." However, in deference and respect to these audiences, I capitalize "Black" when referring to women of African descent. Similar respect is used in reference to "White" women.

Latino/Latina and Hispanic are used interchangeably throughout this book. However, I prefer the use of the term *Latina* to refer to women of Mexican, Puerto Rican, Cuban, Central American, Dominican, or South American heritage and therefore use this term more frequently.

Asian American, Asian/Pacific Islander, Hawaiian, and Asian Pacific

American are used interchangeably to refer to Asians in the United States. Importantly, Asian Americans include persons of Chinese, Filipino, Asian Indian, Korean, Vietnamese, Japanese, Hawaiian, and Pacific Islander ancestry.

The terms *Caucasian, White,* and *European* are used to describe women of European heritage who may be immigrants or U.S. born citizens.

Other women of color—Native American, Native Alaskan, Middle Eastern, and Eastern European—are noted in this book, although the focus is on Latina, Black, and Asian women.

My intent is not to disparage any one group over another or to suggest, in any way, that women of different ethnic and cultural backgrounds should not align themselves or coalesce with other women around common global issues. My sole intent is to raise awareness of the unique cultural and ethnic differences apparent among women and to discuss how these differences impact the success of marketing, sales, and recruitment strategies directed to these audiences.

Introduction

THIS IS A BOOK about a big, virtually uncontested, trillion-dollar consumer market—a market with a population as large as Spain, Italy, or the United Kingdom. It seeks to raise the awareness of corporate America to the business opportunity represented by ethnically and culturally diverse women. It challenges paradigms and dispels myths about women as one, single monolithic group. It is designed to rally the consciousness of Latina, Black, and Asian women to the strategic role they play and will continue to play in fueling the economic engine of American industry—as consumers, as employees, and as entrepreneurs. It celebrates the many "voices" of women—the young, the immigrant, the housekeeper, the affluent, the college student, the business executive, the emerging and successful entrepreneur, the single head-of-household mother, the widow, the aging parent, and more.

Fundamentally, this is a book that seeks to communicate—with respect to all—that marketing to women does not mean marketing to White women alone. It seeks to broaden the thinking of its readers to the impact that culture and ethnicity have in marketing strategy for women consumers. It offers a window into the world of diversity and gender.

The passion driving this book

I am *deeply* passionate about the topic of women and women of color, about celebrating the strength and power of these women, and about helping marketers bridge gaps in brand communication, product development, promotional programs, media considerations, and sales strategies to reach this dynamic and continuously evolving audience.

According to the U.S. Census, women of color are growing in population three times faster than all other women and they have reached critical mass with a U.S. population of 54 million. They generate $1 trillion as consumers and an additional $230 billion as entrepreneurs, and they've exceeded their male counterparts in educational attainment at both the undergraduate and graduate levels. And, with the unprecedented move of a Black woman serving as the First Lady in the White House in 2009, women of color are clearly breaking new ground!

They are incredibly *complex*. Latinas are represented by: foreign born, U.S. born, acculturated, retro-acculturated, unacculturated, Spanish dominant, English dominant, bi-lingual, Mexicans, Cubans, Puerto Ricans, Dominicans, Central Americans, Latin Americans, and according to some experts, women from Spain. African-American women are largely identified as U.S.-born women of African ancestry. However, there is a growing and culturally distinct group of African-descended women emigrating from the continent of Africa to the United States. This group comes to America with the highest level of academic achievement of any immigrant group—European or otherwise. The African-descended group includes Afro-Latina women (my peer group and an audience that can be included among Hispanics or among women of African descent) as well as Afro-Caribbean women (from Jamaica, Haiti, Trinidad, Tobago, the Bahamas, Barbados, Antigua, and other islands in the Caribbean). Each is unique and not to be confused with the values and aspirations of African-American women.

Like Hispanic women, Asian-American women are represented by foreign born, and U.S. born, but have cultural, language, and custom distinctions based on their Chinese, Filipino, Asian Indian, Korean, Vietnamese, Japanese, and other Pacific Islander heritage. They are a rich and highly educated audience whose values of tightly knitted family cohesion, respect for elders, the avoidance of family shame, collectivism, and achieving one's "personal best" are cultural hallmarks of distinction.

Our cultural and ethnic differences shape how we respond to life experiences—a first date, leaving home, exploring career choices, marriage, divorce, giving birth, caring for aging parents, our own aging, and learning how to survive loss. The convergence of gender, diversity, and life stage impact our response to each life event. In addition, women of all colors react differently to messages and product offerings in color cosmetics, skin care, body care, apparel, fashion accessories, and other physical-enhancement products and services. One size truly does *not* fit all in the world of diversity and gender.

What I bring to the discussion of women and women of color

My long-held ambition is to see companies embrace our cultural and ethnic uniqueness as women of all colors with the same tenacity, commitment to grow, and deployment of economic resources that are given to other consumer audiences. I want to encourage discussions that shed light on the contributions made by women of color to a wide range of industries—from cosmetics to cars. I want to underscore the future dependency companies will have on growing market share by appealing not only to women, but also to women of *all* colors. I want to encourage a rational discussion on budget resource allocation to reach this audience and share "best practice" strategies to both engage us as consumers as well as to recruit and retain us as employees. I want to move women of color from the *fringes* of business planning to the *main stage*.

It's not an easy task. I've been committed to marketing to women and to women of color for my entire professional career. Coming out of Columbia University's Graduate School of Business with an MBA in Marketing and moving up and through the ranks of Fortune 100 consumer packaged goods and automotive companies, I sat at the decision-making table as head of marketing and head of diversity, marshaled the troops to create advertising that persuades and connects with women audiences, launched new products to appeal to our unique needs, designed merchandising strategies to target our buying preferences, developed sales training to help retail teams understand how to sell more effectively to us, fought for budget to drive results, created measurement tools to track progress in growing market share, and executed these marketing programs in a way that generated incremental sales and a new profit stream for corporations.

I've had a front row seat in participating in marketing strategy and leading business planning efforts to help brands increase their relevance and appeal to women buyers. And that's true whether the focus has been on marketing cosmetics, skin care, snack foods, children's products, or cars and trucks. I've gained tremendous clarity on what drives a woman to research for months, search the web for hours, and unashamedly ask friends, colleagues and associates—her personal "board of directors"—for their views on the "perfect" new crossover vehicle, the ideal financial planner, or the best restaurant to host an important meeting. I also understand what excites that same methodical woman to go out and impulsively spend $500 on a fabulous new pair of red pumps—a pair of shoes she may only wear once. I know what makes her "tick."

I learned about marketing from the best. Joyce Roché, Harriet Edelman, and Judy Hu are all role models from my days at Avon Products, Inc. and General Motors Corporation. They are, in my opinion, the "best of best." And, as a marketing executive who has managed the P&L for flagship brands at Johnson & Johnson, Clairol, and Avon, I have experience in how to translate these customer insights into marketing plans that deliver results. My most recent corporate experience at General Motors as Executive Director, Diversity Marketing and Sales Strategy provided me with an aerial view of the overarching strategies required to drive success among diverse ethnic groups—the consumer segments that, when combined, account for over 60 percent of all new vehicle sales. The result of our diversity marketing and sales work at GM was an increase in ethnic automotive sales in key divisions and geographic markets for three consecutive years, and in a highly competitive business environment. Women account for the lion's share of the new vehicle buyer, with over 45 percent of sales generated by women buyers and 85 percent of all sales influenced by this group.

My work at Avon Products, Inc., as General Manager for the Women of Color Business unit also provided me with relevant experience on how to grow multicultural sales in the direct-selling industry through targeted recruiting efforts, new product development work, merchandising strategies, grass roots promotions, and advertising and media planning. The result of our work at Avon was a dramatic turnaround in market share and a positive 14-point swing in sales growth among

African-American women—the largest ethnic contributing segment for Avon at that time.

My passion for the topic of marketing to women and women of color is also personal. As a Latina with roots in Santurce, Puerto Rico, I understand the unique traditions that define being Hispanic. I love our music, our language, our strong family traditions, and without question, our food! And, because I am an Afro Latina, a descendant of slaves brought to the New World to work the sugar cane, coffee, and tobacco fields of Puerto Rico, I also deeply understand the challenges and hopes of what it means to be Black. I straddle both worlds, living in what Dr. Marta Vega, President and Founder of the Caribbean Cultural Center calls, "the invisible world" of Afro-descended Spanish, French, and English-speaking people who now—due to immigration trends—represent an "invisible" but growing consumer economy. I have a particularly unique view of the business opportunity associated in reaching the $400 billion U.S.-Afro-Latino or Black-Spanish "segment within a segment," a population nearly as large as that of the Asian-American market. Sadly, few, if any companies recognize this niche segment and fewer still recognize the buying power generated by men and women of African descent who share a common Hispanic ancestry through origins in Cuba, Puerto Rico, the Dominican Republic, Central America, Latin America, and Mexico. My goal is to unveil the business potential of this audience and of others like it.

As CEO of The 85% Niche, I focus my professional and personal experiences to help companies tap into the power of *all* women—White, Black, Latina, Asian, Native American, Middle Eastern, and more—and across many industries through savvy marketing and sales strategies. My goal is to dispel the notion that women are a "niche"; we are a powerful group of consumers capable of generating significant business results.

Why you should read this book

Despite the focus on women and ethnic consumers that has emerged in recent years, I was surprised that there has been no focus on the impact of gender and diversity on business planning, especially on a market segment that rivals the size of Brazil and exceeds that of Mexico in Gross Domestic Product (GDP). Up until now, if corporations have taken the lead in developing initiatives targeted to women, it has done been with a view of women as a monolithic group. Women of color and women of different cultural backgrounds have been grouped together with White women and viewed on the basis of gender identity alone, disregarding the ethnic, cultural, and socioeconomic factors that differentiate female buyers. Similarly, if corporations have adopted "diversity" as a strategy to grow market share, it has most often been applied from the perspective of male and female buyers, minimizing the role that gender plays in brand consideration.

Given the growing population and buying power of women of color, companies need to take a hard look at who constitutes their "women's market," drill deeper, and understand the insights driving behavior and preferences among these unique and evolving female consumers.

The 85% Niche: The Power of Women of All Colors was written to raise awareness around the diversity of women, to show corporate America how to reach these women, and how to do so in a way that yields exceptional revenue and profits. This book also underscores the critical role that an integrated diverse workforce plays in driving exceptional performance. In today's tight labor market, with leading-edge baby boomers approaching retirement, corporations must attract enough talent and human resources to sustain company growth. Women, whose educational attainment levels are at an all-time high and whose management styles are inherently more collaborative than men's, are premiere recruiting targets. Diverse women of color cannot to be overlooked in this discussion.

The basis for knowledge: Methodology

The core of this book's information is my proprietary *Leading Voices* research, a marketing tool designed to hear the "voices" of women globally. *Leading Voices* provide original insights based on: 1) what's relevant and important to women in general, Latina women, Black women of the Diaspora, Chinese, Korean, Asian Indian and other Asian women;

2) physiological differences and how this impacts product decisions— from cosmetics, to skin care, to hair care and apparel, to pharmaceutical products; 3) cultural differences and the desire to see their images and traditions (language, music, art, food, values and spirituality) reflected back to them in the products and services they purchase for themselves and their families; and, 4) the educational, financial, and personal aspirations of women and how this impacts their decisions to enter and remain in the workforce, their selection of products, and their expectations in customer service. *The 85% Niche* conducted original research, including nearly 200 one-on-one interviews with industry thought leaders and consumers to distill key insights on women and women of color. Data mining of existing research on women, diversity, and various economic and census reports were also used to gather facts for this book.

What's in this book and why you need it

The 85% Niche: The Power of Women of All Colors is the definitive book on women of color and marketing to women of color. It provides significant proof supporting the trillion dollar economic buying power of women of color, the rapid demographic growth trends of multicultural women, and the fact that many industries are increasingly dependent upon the purchase decisions of Latina, Black, and Asian women for sales growth. Companies that are "on the fence" regarding whether or not they should focus on women of color will be challenged to rethink their strategies or risk significant lost business from this emerging, influential audience.

Part One of this book is written to provide important quantitative information on the demographics, size, economic buying power, educational attainment levels, geographic trends, and workforce projections for the women's market and for women of color. This section provides basic background information and key factual data and frames the size and opportunity associated with marketing to women of color. Once you complete this section, any doubts you may have had about the economic vibrancy of women of color will be completely dismantled.

Part Two provides an introspective look at each of the major women's ethnic and cultural market segments: specifically, Latinas, Black, and Asian women. Sub-segments of women, such as Caribbean, Afro-Latinas, Puerto Ricans, Cubans, Mexicans, Chinese, and Japanese, are explored from a cultural and demographic point of view. This section also provides compelling marketplace data on the size of the female diversity market, and the impact of immigration trends on ethnic and cultural diversity in the United States. It identifies those industries whose businesses are most dependent upon the purchases by diverse women and demonstrates, how, in the absence of overt marketing initiatives to reach these women, *future market share growth is at risk.*

Part Three delves more deeply into the impact of life stage on gender and diversity. All women—regardless of ethnicity and culture—share a great deal in common and experience many of the same life events, but culture and ethnicity play key roles in how we experience these moments and how we respond to the challenges associated with each life event. This section of the book focuses on the issues that mothers of color and entrepreneurial women of power encounter—issues that are unique to their culture, gender, and life stage.

The practical application of the book, Part Four, introduces the new principles of diversity and gender-centric marketing through case studies in three distinct industries: automotive, personal care, and financial products. The case studies provide the reader with actionable ideas for applying insights about the women's market to his or her own business.

Worksheets and thought-starter exercises are selectively provided throughout the pages of this book to transition the insights and learning to a practical implementation mode. My goal is to stimulate you with new insights and a fresh perspective while also giving you some specific action tools you can immediately integrate into your day-to-day activities. I think you will be surprised to see how small precision-like changes in your marketing and sales plans can have a dramatic impact on your business performance and how these changes can lead to new avenues to brand equity, consideration, and sales.

Top Takeaways

The 85% Niche: The Power of Women of All Colors will stimulate your business plans and provide you with an entirely new view of the market potential of the women's market. You will challenge your marketing teams and advertising agencies to dig deeper, push the envelope, and be relentless in ensuring *all women of all colors* are actively targeted for stronger business performance.

- Women of color are more than just a number. Supported correctly with the right business strategies, the $1 trillion Latina, Black, and Asian women's markets will re-invigorate your business for years to come with brand loyalty and positive word-of-mouth endorsement.

- Women of color are a vital source of employment and entrepreneurial energy. They represent critical talent at the entry, middle management, senior executive leadership, and independent distributor and entrepreneurial levels.

- Effectively marketing to women of color requires an expert understanding of gender marketing, diversity marketing, and life-stage marketing and the matrix created among the disciplines.

- Unleashing the power of women and diversity in your organization is the fastest track to sales growth, share dominance, and profit improvement. Often, diverse groups are the "hidden," underserved audience that is simply waiting for the right invitation to join your brand. The sheer weight of the demographics of these women—now and for many years to come—and their economic power will yield significant incremental sales to your current base of customers.

- Women's marketing strategies and women-of-color diversity strategies can co-exist. Similarly, your male "core" market and women's market can operate simultaneously. This is not a "zero sum," "either/or" game. The harsh realities of our economic times demand a parallel strategy of growth among *all* viable audiences to maximize sales.

- As compelling as the women-of-color opportunity is, it will only succeed if it is measured and tracked, and carries the executive sanction and consistent attention of the senior-most officers of the corporation. Anything less will result in missed opportunities.

I leave you with an open door and desire to hear from you with questions, personal stories, and successes. This is a $1 trillion audience that can turn around and revitalize declining sales performance. It is a dynamic and rapidly growing audience that will, someday, be your majority customer. Knowing how to appeal to her sensibilities will put you in a stronger position to establish brand equity. Contact me at *mmuley@85percentniche.com.* I want to hear from you as you take your business to higher heights of success with this powerful *85% Niche.*

PART ONE
The Foundation

ONE

Economic Opportunity #1: Women

THE RISE in the power of the women's market was anything but smooth. For years women were overlooked as inconsequential to the bottom line, tertiary, and apolitical in their views. Companies dismissed their significance and economic impact. They delegated the women's market to teams outside the core group, creating a disconnected and silo-approach in growing the women's market. States Delia Passi, CEO of Medelia Communications, a company that specializes in selling to women:

> "My take is that corporations are comfortable in the way they do business. Historically, they worked with advertising agencies that provided demographics and the research to develop creative and direct response programs to drive the customers. They didn't create enterprise-wide programs [with women in mind] . . . It's like a family . . . if you bring a new child into the family and only one parent decides to nurture the child, the child suffers. That will be a dysfunctional child [and a dysfunctional family]."

Dysfunctional attempts at marketing to women seem to have been the norm in the past. Because women were not understood or embraced for the vast power and decision-making influence they represent, companies missed the fact that women were changing at a dramatic pace. How they shop, what motivates them to buy, and what are the best ways to reach them are all questions that early marketers failed to ask. They assumed they knew the answers. In some cases, companies ignored the women's market for fear that too much attention would alienate their masculine "core" buyers. In other cases, those companies who ventured to appeal to women made serious mistakes along the way, diluting the impact of their brand messages, promotional programs, or product innovation strategies.

The truth about pink

One failed case that is often cited is in the automotive industry. In the 1950s companies sought to appeal to women by literally making their brands "pink": softer, more feminine versions of the real thing. If the designers of the so-called automobiles for women back in the 1950s had listened to their customers they might not have strayed so far away from what women wanted. They might have understood that women weren't really looking for pink cars equipped with matching cosmetics, umbrellas, and shoulder bags. The 1955 Dodge *La Femme* wore an exterior paint scheme of heather rose and sapphire white, and an interior of coordinated rose jacquard fabrics, complete with feminine accessories like a matching handbag. Sounds lovely, but the product failed miserably. The automotive industry is all about torque, engine, performance, horsepower, and style. It's no wonder the pink campaign of the 1950s failed.

When it comes to pink, the truth is that pink lacks the intensity of true color. It is a *dilution* of color. The psychology of using a diluted, inauthentic, softer version of a product to appeal to a growing economic powerhouse consumer base is indicative of how far removed the automotive industry was from the realities of women. Women—especially women of today—want the "high touch," a personal connection with a brand. They don't want the "pink touch," a diluted attempt at relevancy.

Brand-name selections for 1950's automobiles also went too far in trying to appeal to women. Witness the Pontiac *Parisienne*, the Chevrolet Impala *Martinique*, the Cadillac Eldorado Seville *Baroness,* and of course, the Dodge *LaFemme*. These names stretched the limits of what was appropriate for women who were in the 1950s, by and large, not looking to stand out, but to stand behind their defined roles of the time as homemaker, mother, and wife.

States Anne Doyle, CEO of Anne Doyle Strategies, a communications, media, and leadership coaching company, and former executive at Ford Motor Company:

> "There were decades of inauthentic marketing and advertising to women. [I recall] my years at Ford Motor Company, where companies would give all of this data saying that women did not want to be separated out, that they did not want to have distinction. They went back to pink cars with pink umbrellas . . . and women rejected this. Men were in the room saying that women did not want to be talked to differently. I would sit in that room and every fiber would jump out. Fortunately, I'm thrilled to see that companies are finally starting to get it."

Mistakes in timing

If the automotive industry was listening to its customers in the 1950s it might have understood that while women were just beginning to *think* about flexing their independence, the majority were full-time, at-home mothers. Only 34 percent of women in the 1950s were in the labor force (compared with today's labor force participation rate of 62 percent). Women had not yet benefited from the civil rights or women's movements, from legislation promoting equal opportunity in employment, from delaying child bearing until later in life, or from remaining in school longer to pursue college and post graduate degrees. These socio-political dynamics paved the way for more women working outside the home, and ultimately for women gaining more personal power, more independence, and greater economic freedom.

Had the automotive industry waited until the 1970s to target independent-minded and fashion conscious women, using marketing that did not marginalize the audience, they might have been more successful in selling accessorized vehicles. Recall the great success of Virginia Slims in the 1970s with the "You've Come a Long Way, Baby" campaign and thin, long, feminine cigarettes. Or, the Revlon "Charlie" campaign for fragrance during this same time period.

Fortunately, GM, Ford, Chrysler and others in the automotive industry ultimately learned that the real secret of what women want in automobiles is great product delivered in an *intelligent way*. They are looking for the same high-level features that appeal to all consumers: beautiful design, outstanding quality, great performance, and both personal and environmental safety. And, where differences are needed, for example in height and stature, automotive companies respond by using adjustable pedals to provide a more custom fit. They offer additional storage features in vehicles to meet the needs of larger families. And, safety, an important feature for women automotive buyers, is provided in the engineering and technology features of the vehicle such as: GM's StabiliTrak Electronic Control Stability System, OnStar by GM, and Ford's SYNC Voice Command, a fully-integrated, voice-activated in-car communications and entertainment system. These features are promoted through advertising, reinforced in product sales training, and promoted during test drives and local events.

Mistakes in advertising

Advertising that reinforces patriarchal stereotypes and images of "perfect" women—airbrushed, impossibly unattainable superwomen—is a sure-fired way to ensure failure in marketing to women. Although women place a great deal of importance on image, some advertisers have exploited this and tailored their campaigns and slogans to play off women's insecurities. An example is found in cigarette campaigns.

The Harvard School of Public Health published a research report entitled, "Designing Cigarettes for Women: New Findings from the Tobacco Industry Documents." It reported that tobacco companies use specific strategies to target female consumers. The authors (Carpenter, Wayne, Connolly) conclude that the tobacco industry spends valuable time and resources to target female consumers by taking advantage of female behavior, insecurities, and perception of self-image. To increase sales among women, tobacco companies have developed gender-specific attributions to their products, such as color (pink resurfaces as a key strategy again), flavor, and length. Their attempt to make their products more appealing to women by making them more feminine in style has helped them increase sales nationwide. Carrie Carpenter and her associates write, "These studies demonstrate that marketing strategies, especially for female brands, have contributed to the association of smoking with appealing attributes including female liberation, glamour, success, and thinness."

The tobacco industry is not the only industry that has bet on female stereotypes to boost its sales. Flip though the pages of major magazines, even those designed specifically for women, and you will see that they are filled with ads of thin and impossibly beautiful women wearing designer clothing. Many would argue that the authentic portrayal of women highlighted in the Dove "Real Beauty," the Hanes "Just My Size," or the Playtex Secrets "Who Knows You Like We Do" campaigns are refreshing indications that we are finally on the right track in celebrating the beauty of the "everyday woman." These campaigns are successful in breaking away from stereotypical airbrushed examples of what a woman is supposed to be. They celebrate the honesty of the body and give women freedom to accept beauty in all forms.

Mistakes in selling

For some corporations, failure to connect with women in a meaningful way, or to understand how to approach prospective buyers lies in the sales process. These remarks from Patricia Roberts, former General Director of the Women's Dealer Retail Initiative at General Motors shed light on this topic.

> "The dealership experience can still be a bad one for women because some of the people working in some of the dealerships have difficulty understanding that they need to interact with women as an equal and as a consumer who has buying power. Some salespeople do what is known in the industry as "sidewalk qualifying" which means that they judge the purchasing power by the person's appearance, which by the way, includes gender. Women tend to do more research before they come into the dealership so that they are knowledgeable and able to

interface with a salesperson with intelligence. And some women will bring a male with them so that they feel more comfortable with the purchasing transaction. Until sales people treat all consumers with dignity and respect, the consumer—whether male or female—will be intimidated by the purchase experience."

The automotive industry is not the only industry that has received poor marks in strategies to effectively sell to women. Traditionally male-oriented products and services, such as home buying, banking and financial services, and consumer electronics can benefit from the recognition that women are the majority decision-maker and that a firm handshake, direct eye contact, and respect of her knowledge can be the deal meaker that closes a sale. Part Four of this book provides some examples of companies in these industries that successfully sell to women.

Is the glass half empty or half full?

Companies that want to build relationships with women buyers will want to ask themselves several questions. What changes in their product planning, sales outreach effort, promotional support, messaging, and media mix are required to establish greater relevancy with this multi-trillion dollar audience? Is their current business plan half empty or half full in relation to women buyers?

Eileen Ashley, Senior Vice President for Wealth and Institutional Management at Comerica Bank, a leading financial services company headquartered in Dallas, Texas, had this to say on this question:

"What companies still don't get about the value of the women's market is that you have to change the way you are doing business to really appeal to a diverse segment of consumers. It's not that the glass is half empty or half full; it's just we have to use a **different glass.** Many companies sometimes just don't realize that they may already have the internal assets to appeal to women buyers; they just have to package it differently. Those that struggle keep approaching the market using the same glass—the same strategy—and then wonder why they don't get the results they want."

The wrong glass can take the form of the wrong advertising message, an ineffective media plan, a product that misses the mark, paltry budgets, a sales approach that fails to understand how women want to be treated in the buying process, a corporate infrastructure that is absent women leaders, and more. Using the same "glass" or business plan over and over to reach a fundamentally new audience is not likely to produce the desired results, as Ms. Ashley notes. It's time for business leaders to use a *new set of glassware* and change the way they are doing business, despite the sentimental value associated with the strategies of the past.

The real truth

So, what are the important truths about the women's market? What is her real power? It took years of work and the tireless effort of subject matter experts, academicians, researchers, and economists to prove the case that women are economic opportunity #1. Their extensive and well-documented studies from the fields of biology, psychology, economics, and demographics unequivocally support the vitality and preeminence of the women's market.

It would take many pages to summarize the tomes of work done on the women's market. Here's an aerial view of what experts have learned about women. It's the tip of a massive iceberg that demonstrates the changes taking place among women as a vibrant economic powerhouse.

FACT WOMEN ARE NOT MEN IN DRESSES.

Scientific research proves that our brains are wired differently. Men and women have unique biological and hormonal differences that cause us to react to the same stimuli in unique ways. Women have more dendrites in their brain structure than men. This results in more connections between brain cells and an ability to express ideas more easily. There have been studies to show that women speak an average of 20,000 words per day, compared with only 7,000 words per day spoken by men. We have a great deal to say about virtually every topic and we value the ability to freely express these ideas. It's no wonder that social networking, blogs, and the Internet in general are mainstay tools for women today.

Women also have more *corpus collusum,* the thick network of nerves that connects the right and left hemispheres of the brain, allowing us to move from right brain/creative problem solving to linear/left brain analytical thinking more easily than men. Women are contextual and holistic thinkers.

Women produce more *estrogen,* which creates strong nesting and nurturing feelings. These feelings transcend home and family; in the workplace and as entrepreneurs, women tend to be more involved in the welfare of their employees and teams than men are. Reports by the Center for Women's Business Research, for example, indicate that women entrepreneurs tend to provide more job sharing, flex time, and technology enabled benefits to their employees than male-owned businesses. Women-owned businesses are also more involved in philanthropic giving, another indication of our tendencies to nurture others.

FACT   WOMEN HAVE UNIQUE COMMUNICATION STYLES.

While there are basic biological variants that account for the different ways in which men and women use language, socialization also plays a role in our communication styles. Experts in gender sociology state that the root of language discrepancies stems from childhood experiences and the gender roles children fulfill in the home and school. During childhood, boys and girls belong to two very different subcultures. The behavior of both men and women (as adults) can be pinpointed to their basic experiences in childhood and in their formative adolescent years. M. Talbot, a researcher at the Center for Research in Media and Cultural Studies comments on the different forms of play that boys and girls assume during this phase of life:

> "Boys, who tend to play in large groups with hierarchal social structure, learn to value status and become power-focused; whereas girls, who tend to play in small groups of 'best friends,' learn to value intimacy and become solidarity-focused. In the process, children acquire different gender-appropriate behavior."

As adults, men and women still unconsciously revert to the tendencies instilled in them as youths.

FACT WOMEN USE LANGUAGE TO CREATE AND BUILD RAPPORT.

Women value relationships and the continuous cultivation of new and already established rapports, a value that is reflected in their linguistic choices. Where men can be blunt and direct, women are more aware and conscious of others' emotions. They more often attempt to stop, understand, and analyze situations before forming opinions. Women recognize a gray area in communication, whereas men tend to see things in black and white. They are often more sensitive in their choice of words. Robin Lakoff, in an article entitled "Gender" published in the *Encyclopedia of Language & Linguistics* reported:

> "Women's language included a preference for milder over more strongly tabooed expletives, exaggerated politeness, an elaborate color vocabulary, use of . . . adjectives ('lovely,' 'divine') and intensifiers ('so nice'), hedging to reduce the force of an utterance and/or the speaker's degree of commitment to it, and phrasing statements as questions, using rising intonations and/or end-of-sentence questions tags."

FACT WOMEN'S DECISION-MAKING PROCESSES ARE DIFFERENT FROM MEN'S.

Women have a distinct decision-making approach in comparison with men. According to Marti Barletta, author of *Marketing to Women,* men make decisions in a linear process; women take a spiral approach, always looking for the "perfect" decision. A woman will go through great lengths to research before finalizing a product or service decision that meets her needs. And, even at that point, she will always be open to receiving more information to truly perfect her decision.

We noticed this distinct decision-making pattern at General Motors Corporation. Through research we observed that women desired more uninterrupted quality time on the showroom floor to browse vehicles, investigate the interiors, explore the back seat to see how comfortable their children would be, check the rear view to determine their span of vision, get a first-hand "feel" for being in the driver's seat, and consult with sales managers. Women spent an average of five minutes more in the showroom before buying than men did. However, this additional time paid off. Our studies showed that whereas women spent more time on the showroom floor, they had a higher purchase rate than men did. The lesson: women are deliberate, intentional, and thoughtful in their decision-making styles. Marketers who give them the space and freedom to satisfy their purchase criteria have a higher probability of gaining their business.

▶ *Women feel misjudged and misunderstood*

59% of women feel misunderstood by food marketers.
66% feel misunderstood by health care marketers.
74% feel misunderstood by automotive marketers.
84% feel misunderstood by investment marketers.
91% of women in one survey said that advertisers don't understand them.

Source: M2W

FACT   WOMEN HOLD THE $3.7 TRILLION DOLLAR PURSE STRINGS.

From automotive, to consumer electronics, to home improvement products, to travel, and more, women are the powerhouse consumers that influence either directly, or indirectly, which products and services will be consumed by their families, themselves, and through word-of-mouth, their friends, and associates. Women control $3.7 trillion in purchasing power and have earned a coveted position of leadership on the global map. More specifically, if women were a country they would rank #3, behind the United States and Japan in global GDP.

▶ *Women and money*

Women generate $3.7 trillion in buying power.
Women own 40% of all stocks.
Women head 40% of all high net worth households.

Women aged 24–37 are better prepared for retirement than their male counterparts. They have an average of $410,000 designated for retirement compared with $248,000 for men of the same age group

Sources: U.S. Census, WOW Facts, Allstate

FACT WOMEN DRIVE THE ENTREPRENEURIAL ENGINE OF AMERICA.

Women are essential as consumers and, with $1.9 trillion as entrepreneurs, they are vital as business owners. Looking at the numbers of women entrepreneurs, including the gross sales receipts generated by 50 percent or more women-owned businesses, the sheer magnitude of the influence women hold in business is abundantly clear.

▶ *Women and entrepreneurship*

Women-owned businesses employ 18.5 million workers. That is more than the Fortune 500 combined.

These businesses generate $1.9 trillion in annual sales.

Women own 10.4 million businesses in the U.S. or 41% of all U.S. firms.

This number has almost tripled since 1987, when there were 4.5 million women-owned businesses.

A woman opens a business in the U.S. every 30 seconds.

Source: Center for Women's Business Research

FACT WOMEN HAVE MADE SIGNIFICANT ADVANCES IN EDUCATION.

Women understand that in order to compete in the workplace they must have the training, the credentials, and the springboard that a college and post-graduate degree afford. It's no surprise then that women out-rank the number of men in college by a full six percentage points (57 percent of college students are women; 43 percent are men).

▶ *Women and education*

57% of all Bachelors degrees are awarded to women.

55% of all Masters degrees are awarded to women.

50% of all law school degrees are awarded to women.

42% of all medical degrees are awarded to women.

42% of all Ph.D.s are awarded to women.

Source: U.S. Census Bureau

FACT   WOMEN ARE ADVANCING IN THE WORKPLACE AND IN THE BOARDROOM.

In 1950, only one-third of American women of working age had a paid job. Today twice as many women do, and they make up almost half of America's workforce. In contrast, men's employment rate has slid by 12 percentage points from 89 percent in 1950 to 77 percent today. Almost everywhere more women are employed and the percentage of men with jobs has fallen. The exception is outside the U.S. where women's integration in the workplace still has far to go. For example, in Italy and Japan, women's share of jobs is still 40 percent or less.

According to Catalyst, the leading nonprofit membership organization working globally with businesses and the professions to build inclusive workplaces and expand opportunities for women and business, women are making advancements in the boardroom and are influencing the representation of women in the workforce. Companies with 30 percent women board members in 2001 had, on average, 45 percent *more* women corporate officers by 2006, compared with companies with no women board members. "Women leaders are role models to early- and mid-career women and, simply by being there at the top, encourage pipeline women to aspire to senior positions. They see that their skills will be valued and rewarded," said Ilene H. Lang, President of Catalyst. Moreover, the presence of women on corporate boards has a positive impact on financial performance. Specifically, Catalyst reports that Fortune 500 companies with the largest representation of women board directors and corporate officers achieve, on average, a 35 percent higher return on equity and 34 percent higher total return to shareholders than those with low representation numbers.

▶ *Women and the boardroom*

Women accounted for 23 CEOs of Fortune 1000 companies in 2008. Three were women of color.

Women represented 2.4% of all Fortune 500 CEOs in 2007.

Women accounted for 6.7% of all Fortune 500 top earners in 2007.

Women accounted for 14.8% of all Fortune 500 Board seats in 2007, compared with 12.4% in 2001.

Women accounted for 15.4% of all corporate officers in Fortune 500 companies in 2007, up from 12.5% in 2000.

Sources: DiversityInc., WOW Facts, Catalyst, Women CEO's of the Fortune 1000 (2008)

FACT WOMEN AND POLITICS MIX WELL.

Women are powerful politicians. The 2008 U.S. presidential race cast a bright light on this fact—both in terms of the roles that Senator Hillary Clinton and Governor Sarah Palin played in the voting process, and in the role women played in selecting Barack Obama as the 44TH president of the United States. Although a highly diverse coalition of voters came together to cast their majority vote for Obama, women represented the largest cohort of supporters. According to the Center for American Women and Politics, 56 percent of all women voters supported Obama versus 48 percent of men. Moreover, Obama won across all women groups: Caucasian women (46 percent), African American women (96 percent), and Latina women (68 percent) Asian women voter data was not reported.

In earlier elections and since 1964, women in the United States have voted in higher absolute numbers than men, and the gap has grown steadily. Women began voting at higher rates than men in 1980, and in 2004, the voter turnout rate was 60.1 percent for women compared with 56.3 percent for men, with women outvoting men across every racial and ethnic group. Adding to this, women now are bringing their purses to the polls, making more financial contributions to campaigns. According to the Center for Responsive Politics, women contributed a bigger share of large individual contributions in the 2008 election cycle than at any time since 1989. Female donors gave nearly 30 percent of the money collected in amounts greater than $200 by federal candidates, political action committees and parties, the Center found. Women contributed 26 percent of that money in the 2000 cycle and

24 percent in the 1996 cycle. Although financial contribution reports for the 2008 presidential election by gender were not available at the time of this book's publication, it is likely that women played a key role in the 2008 presidential financial campaign.

FACT WOMEN GATHER INFORMATION DIFFERENTLY THAN MEN.

The Internet plays a major role in the research process for women. Right now, 68 percent of women use the Internet compared with 66 percent of men. Online buying is big business for women, with most preferring to surf the web for information, deals, and ideas on what to buy for themselves, family, and friends. Moreover, women are accessing blogs, social networks, and other community-based media for the ability to quickly connect with like-minded persons. Marketers are taking note. Analyst e-Marketer predicts that by 2011, $4.1 billion will be spent worldwide for social network advertising, a dramatic increase from the $480 million spent in 2006. In 2008 alone, global ad spend in the social networking arena is expected to increase 75 percent year over year, amounting to $2.1 billion.

▶ *Women represent the majority of the online market*

Women generate $46 million in online buying.

68% of all women regularly use the Internet vs. 66% of men.

Source: M2W

FACT WOMEN'S EARNINGS ARE ON THE RISE.

According to the U.S. Census Bureau, the median annual earnings of females over age 15 who work full time and on a year-round basis were $30,203 in 2002. This represents a 1.8 percent increase in real earnings over 2000, adjusting for inflation. Comparable earnings for men increased only 1.4 percent during the same time period. In households where partners work and live together (either married or unmarried), 22 percent of the women make more than their partners by at least

$5,000. Sixty percent of women in households where both individuals are employed earn at least as much as their partners.

FACT **WOMEN ARE THE PRIMARY PURCHASERS.**

Women make hundreds of decisions weekly, if not daily, concerning which products get to enter through the family gate and which are left at the curbside. And even if women don't always sign on the dotted line, they influence the majority of all purchases. How? Women determine which brands enter the "considered set of competitive options"— whether the options are focused on where the family will vacation, where the children will attend school, or which banking institution offers the best personalized service and client consultation. Women decide which brands provide sufficient value to warrant their consideration of options.

▶ *Women influence 85% of all consumer purchases—from autos to health care*

91%	New home purchases
66%	PCs
92%	Vacations
80%	Health care providers
45%	New cars, trucks, and crossover vehicles
89%	Bank accounts
93%	Food & OTC pharmaceuticals

Source: WOW Facts, R.L. Polk

Where do we go from here?

The facts about the women's market speak for themselves. No other consumer group in America has the power, influence, and importance to Fortune 500 corporations that women do. Virtually any company in the 21st century with a new product, service, or idea to sell wants to appeal to women. Most corporations understand the market potential of this audience. Or, at least, they should if they want their business to do well. Take the quiz at the end of this chapter to see if you've mastered the critical facts in relation to the women's market. Each correctly answered question is worth 5 points. If you score below 15 points, go back and re-read this section. You want to make sure you are armed with fundamental insights on the power of women as consumers. If you've scored a perfect score of 25, congratulations! You are ready to move on and learn more. Where, for example, do women of color fit into the equation of the women's market? We examine this central question in the next chapter.

Women as the #1 Powerhouse Consumer
True or False?

1. Women hold the $3.7 trillion purse string.
2. Women have unique communication and relationship styles.
3. Women use language to build rapport.
4. Women are the major purchasers of goods and services.
5. Women's educational attainment is on the rise.

[Answers: Q1. True. Q2. True. Q3. True. Q4. True. Q5. True.]

Let's talk about these points. Send your comments to me at my website: *www.85percentniche.com.* I'd love to hear from you.

TWO

The Power of Women of All Colors

AMERICAN WOMEN have never looked so good! From full-figured to small delicate frames; from olive to cappuccino and warm chocolate skin tones; from tightly curled coifs, to neatly corn-rowed braids, to long, wavy, or silky straight hair; from high cheekbones, to sculpted necklines, the American woman of today is more beautiful, confident, and accomplished than ever before. And, with as much money to spend as the entire gross domestic product of countries such as Spain, Mexico, and Canada, women of color are an economic force to be reckoned with. As Patricia Russell-McCloud, national motivational speaker says: "Women of color are *intentional*; they are *clear*; they are *purposeful*. They are leading the way."

In a nutshell, U.S. women of color are the catalysts of sweeping change across every sector in America. From education, to corporations, to the retail markets, women of color embody determination, a passion to succeed, and the stamina to go the distance. Women of color are taking the lead and doing so in ways that command our attention, despite the long history of disenfranchisement from academic institutions, from the inner circle of boardrooms, and from the impenetrable "old boys network." They are truly the "sweet spot" for the 21st century.

As large as Spain and Italy

With almost 54 million females, or 35.2 percent of the U.S. female population of non-Anglo descent, the "bronzing" of America has resulted in a population of women of color as large as that of many European nations. For comparison purposes, there are more women of color in the U.S. than there are women working full-time, an audience that, according to the U.S. Department of Labor, is comprised of 51 million persons. Over the seven-year period from 2000 to 2007, the population of women of color grew 18.7 percent while the non-Hispanic White female population experienced relatively flat growth at 1.1 percent. In general, women of color grew *three times faster* than all women from 2000 to 2007, with Latinas and Asian-American women driving most of that growth.

▶ **Figure 2.1   Growth among U.S. females, 2000–2007**

Segments	2007	2000	% Growth
Latina	21,980,731	17,144,023	28.2%
Black	21,286,017	19,461,176	9.4
Asian American	8,291,405	6,623,231	25.2
Asian	*7,784,432*	*6,172,636*	*26.1*
Native Hawaiian/Pacific Islander	*506,973*	*450,595*	*12.5*
American Indian/Native Alaskan	2,292,162	2,136,916	7.3
Total women of color *(Includes all females of color in U.S.)*	**53,850,315**	**45,365,346**	**18.7**
All Other (Non-Hispanic White) Females	99,111,944	98,002,997	1.1
Total U.S. Females	152,962,259	143,368,343	6.7

Source: U.S. Census Bureau

Eighty-eight percent of the absolute growth in the U.S. female population from 2000 to 2007 was attributable to women of color. Specifically, of the 9.6 million females added to the U.S. population during this time period, 8.5 million were Latina, Black, Asian, Pacific Islander, Native American, or Alaska Natives. Higher fertility rates, immigration trends, and the aging of the general market resulted in nine out of every ten females added to the women's population being women of color. That's hugely important for companies whose products and services are dependent on women—cosmetics, health and beauty aids, fashion, as well as traditionally male-dominated products such as cars, trucks, financial services, electronics, and more. The demographic changes among women of color are creating a massive and seismic shift in the women's market.

▶ Figure 2.2   Population change, U.S. women, 2000–2007

Segments	2007	2000	Population change	% Growth
Total women of color *(Includes all females of color in U.S.)*	53,850,315	45,365,346	8,484,969	18.7%
All other females	99,111,944	98,002,997	1,108,947	1.1
Total U.S. females	152,962,259	143,368,343	9,593,916	6.7

Source: U.S. Census Bureau

THINK ABOUT IT

Knowing that 9 out of 10 new females in this country are Latina, Black or Asian, how does this affect your decisions about:

Your Product Portfolio

What enhancements to your current product line are necessary to appeal to the changing demographics of your customer base?

Your Communication Message

How do you ensure that your message resonates in the language and with the cultural cues that connect with women of color? Do you work with ethnic agency specialists? How does your mainstream agency integrate with your diversity teams?

Your Budgets

Are you spending in line with who the ultimate customer is? Are you tracking sales by women of color to determine your level of success? What is your share of voice relative to competition among women of color?

Your Workforce

Are you working to create a workforce that mirrors the customer market? Who are your top women-of-color performers? Do you personally know them and support their career growth?

Black women are almost as large a group as the U.S. Latina population

Within the women-of-color market, Latinas continue to represent the largest audience, although not to the same degree that we see in broader multicultural population reports. There are only slightly more Latinas in this country than there are African-American women. Due to immigration and the propensity of men of color to immigrate to this country in larger numbers than women of color, the ratio of Hispanic and Asian-American men to women is higher than the ratio of Black or Native American men to women. Figure 2.3 below shows the share of each group among all U.S. women.

▶ Figure 2.3   Women of color as a share of all U.S. women

	2007	% Total women
Latina	21,980,731	14.4%
Black	21,286,017	13.9
Asian American	8,291,405	5.4
Asian	7,784,432	5.1
Native Hawaiian/Pacific Islander	506,973	0.3
American Indian/Native Alaskan	2,292,162	1.5
Total women of color (Includes all females of color in U.S.)	**53,850,315**	**35.2**
All Other Females	99,111,944	64.8
U.S. Females	152,962,259	100.0

Source: U.S. Census Bureau

From a segment perspective, Latinas represent 41 percent of all women of color, African-American women represent nearly 40 percent of the total, Asian-American women account for slightly more than 15 percent, and American Indian/Native Alaskan women represent the remaining 4 percent.

▶ Figure 2.4   Segments, women of color

U.S. females of color	% Total women of color
Latina	40.8%
Black	39.5

U.S. females of color	% Total women of color
Asian American	15.4
Asian	*14.5*
Native Hawaiian/Pacific Islander	*0.9*
American Indian/Native Alaskan	4.3
Total women of color *(Includes all females of color in U.S.)*	100.0

Source: U.S. Census Bureau

There will continue to be record growth in the women of color population over the next several years, with the current 54 million women of color population increasing to 63 million by 2020, 75 million by 2030 and ultimately to over 100 million—or half of the U.S. female population by 2050 or sooner. According to U.S. Census Bureau projections, the number of non-Hispanic White females will essentially remain flat through 2040 and begin to decline in population by 2050.

▶ Figure 2.5 Projected growth of U.S. women 2020–2050

U.S. females	2020	2030	2040	2050
Total women of color *(Includes all females of color in U.S.)*	63,057,000	75,107,000	88,459,000	102,254,000
(Non-Hispanic White) Females	103,014,000	104,660,000	104,977,000	104,386,000
U.S. Females	166,071,000	179,767,000	193,436,000	206,640,000

Source: U.S. Census Bureau

Women of color are young, offering greater lifetime value— as customers and as employees

Women of color are on average eleven years younger than non-Hispanic White females. Their median age is 31 years compared with 42 years for all U.S. females. With these additional eleven years comes the opportunity to generate more sales over the lifetime of the customer, who, as you shall read later, is a disproportionate and heavy user of many disposable products and services. From initial product trial, to repeat business, to word-of-mouth referral, women of color offer tremendous advantage and profitability to the retail markets. Every dollar that you spend in the women-of-color market comes back to you exponentially with brand loyalty and with strong word-of-mouth endorsement.

The youthfulness of women of color, coupled with increased levels of educational attainment makes them very attractive from a workforce perspective. Not only will women of color close talent gaps in the workforce pipeline, but also their addition to the management ranks will foster a more dynamic work environment—one that generates greater diversity of strategic thinking and greater productivity.

Other important demographic highlights that validate the youthfulness of the women-of-color market include the following:

- Thirty percent of all women of color are under age 18 compared with 20 percent of non-Hispanic White women;

- Forty-one percent of women of color are in the critical 18-to-44 age segment, compared with 34 percent of non-Hispanic White women;

- There are half as many women of color over age 65 as there are non-Hispanic White women—8 percent vs. 17 percent, respectively; and,

- Latinas are the youngest of all women of color, with a median age of 28 years, followed by African-American women, 32 years; Native American and Alaskan Natives, 32.5 years; and Asian/ Pacific Islanders, 35 years.

▶ Figure 2.6   Age of U.S. females by segment, 2007

	Hispanic	Black	Asian/ Pacific Is.	Nat. Amer./ Alaskan	Women of color	Non-Hisp. White
Females	21,980,731	21,286,017	8,291,405	2,292,162	53,850,315	101,346,238
Under 18 years	**34.3%**	**29.0%**	**24.5%**	**26.4%**	**30.4%**	**20.2%**
Under 5 years	10.9	8.2	7.2	5.7	9.1	5.4
5 to 13 years	16.5	14.0	12.1	13.3	14.6	9.9
14 to 17 years	6.9	6.8	5.2	7.4	6.7	4.9
18 to 64 years	**59.2%**	**61.4%**	**66.1%**	**64.5%**	**61.4%**	**62.4%**
18 to 24 years	10.9	10.8	9.2	12.4	10.7	8.7
25 to 44 years	31.3	28.3	33.8	28.2	30.4	25.4
45 to 64 years	17.0	22.3	23.1	23.9	20.3	28.3

	Hispanic	Black	Asian/ Pacific Is.	Nat. Amer./ Alaskan	Women of color	Non-Hisp. White
65 years +	6.5	9.6	9.4	9.1	8.2	17.4
Median age	27.8	32.0	34.6	32.5	31.2	42.1

Source: U.S. Census Bureau

Women of color have one trillion dollars in buying power

The buying power of women of color surged from $200 billion in 1990 to nearly $1 trillion in 2007. By 2010, the buying power of women of color will rise to $1.2 trillion—a 20 percent increase over 2007 levels.

Women of color earn more and own more than at any other time in recorded history and there is no evidence of progress slowing down. All indications point to continued growth in economic strength. Our spending power is comparable in size to the gross domestic product of South Africa, Saudi Arabia, and Switzerland—combined! It is as large as the GDP of Spain, Mexico, and Canada, ranking U.S. women of color #10 as a global economy. We account for 27 percent of the $3.7 trillion buying power of *all* women in this country. Among all persons of color, women hold 44 percent of the $2.7 trillion multicultural wallet projected in the year 2010. And, for perspective, by 2010 women of color's $1.2 trillion buying power will begin to approach the $1.6 trillion controlled by the 82 million mothers in this country who work. That's *power.*

In short, women of color are generating more disposable income than their history, length of residence in this country, language, and access to education would suggest possible. They are producing more wealth and doing so at a rate that exceeds their population growth. Given the historical challenges of disenfranchisement in the educational sector and in corporate America, these are outstanding results that should be celebrated. Women of color have transcended many institutional roadblocks and continue to do so in a way that commands the serious attention of marketers and businesses.

▶ Figure 2.7   Women of color population and buying power

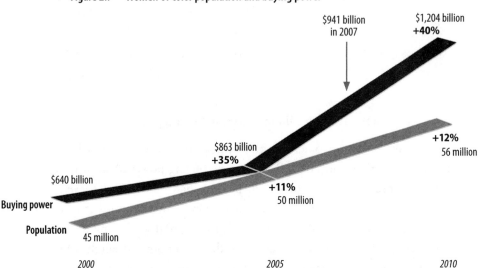

Source: U.S. Census Bureau, Selig Center

Super-affluent households

The affluence of the diverse markets and the control held by women of color in managing these households represents yet another opportunity for marketers. According to the *Statistical Abstract of the United States,* 2.3 percent of all U.S. households earn incomes in excess of $200,000 per year. Approximately 14 percent of these "super-affluent" homes are diverse. Based on projections of the numbers of U.S. households in this income bracket for the year 2010, and given the rapid acceleration of demographics, education, employment, and entrepreneurship among persons of color, approximately 18 percent of these homes, or 525,000 households, will be a diverse family, or a "family of color."

Women of color, by virtue of their strong influence in family decision-making, will be at the helm of these super-affluent homes. Given a minimum $200,000 annual household income, this translates to a segment that generates $105 billion every year. Prestige automotive, retirement, financial wealth-building services, vacation home purchases, fine jewelry, couture fashion, cruise and airline travel, luxury hotels, insurance, college and education planning are among the many products and services appealing to this high-end audience of families of color. These families are wealthier and committed to living life to its full potential. They now have the economic means to do so. They are vested in their financial wellbeing and view money as a tool to help them achieve their life goals.

▶ Figure 2.8   Affluence of U.S. households, by diversity

	Total U.S.	Asian-American	Hispanic	African-American
Median household income	$42,409	$52,626	$33,103	$29,026
$250,000 +	1.3%	2.0%	0.5%	0.4%
$200,000 – 249,000	1.0	2.1	0.4	0.4
$75,000 – 199,000	22.8	30.7	13.7	12.2
$50,000 – 74,999	18.3	18.9	16.8	13.9
$35,000 – 49,999	15.1	13.6	16.4	14.8
$25,000 – 34,999	12.2	10.5	15.7	14.5
$10,000 – 24,999	20.2	14.3	25.5	26.1
Less than $10,000	9.1	7.9	11.0	17.7

Source: U.S. Census Bureau, *Statistical Abstract of the U.S., "Income, Expenditure, and Wealth, 2002"*

Among women of color, more are single

Single women made headline news in 2005 when, for the first time, married couples became a minority in American households. According to the U.S. Census Bureau report, tens of thousands of women are divorced every year and many live alone.

While this was cause for news in the general market, this is not revolutionary in the women-of-color market segment. Owing primarily to the large numbers of African-American women who are not married and the youthfulness of the women-of-color market, more than half—55.8 percent—of all women of color are single. This includes divorced, widowed, and never married women aged 15 and older. Women of color are younger, more self-dependent, and less reliant on a mate for their economic well being than their Caucasian counterparts. Sometimes they have not had any other option. They have had to learn *how* to be Chief Operating Officer of their homes, *how* to care for their children, and *how* to juggle the demands of life without a partner long before it was a mainstream phenomenon.

Four in ten American single women are not White

Single women of color are also disproportionately representative of the entire single women's market. According to the U.S. Census Bureau, there are approximately 22 million divorced, separated, widowed, and never-married women of color over age 15. By comparison, there are 51 million non-Hispanic White women over age 15 who are in the same marital status. Therefore, *43 percent of all single women are women of color.* This figure is disproportionately higher than the 35.2 percent share that women of color represent of the U.S. women's market population—almost ten percentage points higher.

▶ Figure 2.9   Marital status of U.S. women over age 15, 2007

Marital status	Hispanic	Black	Asian/ Pacific Is.	Nat. Amer./ Alaskan	Women of color	Women 15+
Married	50.9%	31.2%	60.0%	43.5%	44.2%	52.2%
Divorced	8.8	12.8	5.4	13.7	10.1	10.8
Widowed	5.6	10.4	6.9	7.4	7.8	10.5
Separated	4.6	5.9	1.6	3.7	4.6	2.5
Never Married	30.1	39.7	26.1	31.7	33.5	24.0
Total Single	49.1	68.8	40.0	56.5	55.8	47.8

Source: U.S. Census Bureau

THINK ABOUT IT

According to the U.S. Census, there are approximately 22 million divorced, separated, widowed, and never-married Latina, Black, and Asian women in the U.S.

Living Alone and In Control

They are calling the shots and making decisions on their own. Are you helping them make informed decisions about your brands?

Single Women of Color are a Gold Mine

These 22 million control *all* spending decisions in their households. How much of their business are you leaving on the table by not courting them as customers?

- *56% of women of color (aged 15+) are single.*
- *43% of all U.S. single women are women of color.*

Driving the purchase decisions

How do women of color, as a group, impact consumption in some of the largest U.S. industries? Let's start with the automotive industry.

Automotive

According to Marc Bland, Manager–Analytical Solutions and Multi-Cultural Lead at R. L. Polk, women of color are key contributors to the upward trend in female automotive market share. The combined automotive purchases of Black, Latina, and Asian women represent approximately 22 percent of new vehicles registered by all women. However, Mr. Bland notes this figure as a conservative number for two reasons:

1. Gender of the household head is not necessarily the share of the "drivers" who are women; and,

2. African American registrations are slightly undercounted by approximately 4 percentage points.

Given these factors, 25 to 26 percent of all new vehicle registrations among women are estimated to be made to women of color and a much higher percentage actually drive these new cars and trucks.

Relative to men, women of color are out-gaining men of color in share of new vehicle registrations. Based on R. L. Polk's July 2008 calendar-year-to-date new vehicle registrations, women of color increased their share of the ethnic automotive market by 2 percentage points—from 40.1 percent in 2003 to 41.9 percent in 2008 while men of color declined from 59.9 percent in 2003 to 58.1 percent in 2008. Against a retail universe of 15 million new vehicle buyers, the author estimates that women of color represent upwards of 1.8 million new car and truck unit sales. At an average price tag of $30,000 each, diverse women, as a group, represent a $54 billion automotive market. Although future predictions in the automotive industry are difficult, this figure may grow to 2.1 million new vehicle unit sales by 2010, or $63 billion. The question automotive manufacturers must ask, is "What is the impact to my top line and bottom line sales if I don't create an integrated plan that leverages women of color." This $54 billion market is too large to ignore.

Food and beverage

Latinas spend $64 billion on food annually, a number driven by the population and larger household sizes. Importantly, 77 percent of Latinas state, "Food is a source of pleasure in my life." African-American women spend $57 billion on food-related items and skew high on food-at-home expenditures ($36 billion) as a percent of their overall spending, (Selig Center, Consumer Expenditure Survey). Latinas and Black women are also significantly more likely than non-Hispanic Whites and younger females to cook and eat at home; there is a preference for traditionally prepared family meals vs. restaurant eating. Some of the reasons are related to economy and cost savings; others are related to the bonding that takes place during the preparation of meals as well as the bonding that occurs at the family dinner table.

Health and beauty products

Black, Latina, or Asian women consume a minimum of 12.5 percent of all health and beauty products. Against an industry estimated at $60 billion (retail), this conservatively translates to a $7.5 billion Health and Beauty category opportunity among diverse women. This includes cosmetics, skin care and hair care products consumed by diverse women. Estimates by *Packaged Facts* indicate this number will grow to over $11 billion by 2010. Clearly, the health and beauty aids industry is a prime industry for the heavy consumption habits and unique beauty needs of women of color.

Financial products and services

Financial institutions have an enormous opportunity to tap into the power and pocketbooks of ethically diverse women. Twenty-three percent of Latinos (vs. 8 percent of non-Hispanic Whites) are "saving to buy a home," and 60 percent of the Spanish-speaking population is "very/somewhat likely" to buy a home in the next three years. However, only 43 percent (vs. 66 percent of non-Hispanic Whites) have traditional savings accounts and only 60 percent (vs. 84 percent of non-Hispanic Whites) have checking accounts. Cash is the preferred form of payment among Latinos, suggesting an opportunity for greater education and new marketing outreach strategies. Fifty-one percent of Hispanics vs. 15 percent of non-Hispanic Whites agree with the statement "cash as the form of payment you use most often for purchases of $100 or more." (Source: Fannie Mae)

▶ Figure 2. 10 Spending by ethnicity, by category

Category	Black	Hispanic	Asian	Total diversity	All consumers	Index diversity to all consumers
Food at home	9.3%	10.4%	7.4%	8.9%	8.3%	107
Food away from home	4.7	6.1	6.6	5.9	5.5	107
Alcoholic beverages	0.6	0.9	0.7	0.7	0.9	78
Housing	37.0	35.6	36.3	36.3	32.4	112
Apparel & Services	5.6	5.1	3.9	4.7	5.0	94
Transportation	17.7	19.6	16.6	17.8	18.5	96
Health care	4.6	4.2	4.4	4.4	5.3	83
Entertainment	3.5	3.6	3.8	3.7	5.2	71
Personal care	1.6	1.4	1.2	1.3	1.5	87
Reading	0.2	0.1	0.2	0.2	0.5	40
Education	1.5	1.4	4.2	2.6	1.6	163
Tobacco products	0.6	0.5	0.3	0.4	0.8	50
Cash contributions	2.9	1.7	2.9	2.5	2.9	86
Personal insurance	8.7	8.2	10.6	9.4	9.3	101
Miscellaneous	1.6	1.2	1.0	1.2	2.4	50

Source: Selig Center for Economic Growth

Geographic markets of major influence

It has been projected that by 2042 half of the U.S. population will be diverse. In states like California, 57 percent of the state's female population today is already diverse. In Texas, 52 percent of the female population is Hispanic, African American, or Asian American. And, in several other states, including New Mexico, Hawaii, and the District of Columbia, women of color represent more than 40 percent of the state's total population.

If you are doing business in any of these states, you have an opportunity to grow sales by recruiting and selling to women of color. I
would encourage you to ensure there is proper business alignment from
a strategy, communication, and financial resource perspective to realize
the full potential of these markets from a woman-of-color view. In fact,
given the rapidly growing population and economic buying power of
women of color, the success of your business will depend upon how
well you reach out to this dynamic group—as consumers, as employees,
and as suppliers of your business.

Here is an aerial view of the major markets where women of color
play a significant role in the overall population of women.

▶ **Figure 2.11 Women of color as share of all women in a state**

women of color as percent of all women

District of Columbia	72%
Hawaii	62
California	57
Texas	52
New Mexico	45
Mississippi	39
New York	37
Maryland	37
Louisiana	37
Georgia	36

Source: U.S. Census Bureau

▶ **Figure 2.12 Top ten states for women of color by population size**

State	Population	% Total
1. California	8,482,484	20.8%
2. Texas	4,810,450	11.8
3. New York	3,617,126	8.8
4. Florida	2,703,457	6.6
5. Illinois	1,936,538	4.7
6. Georgia	1,508,791	3.7
7. New Jersey	1,399,872	3.4
8. North Carolina	1,134,229	2.7
9. Maryland	1,007,829	2.5
10. Michigan	987,329	2.2

Source: U.S. Census 2000

Education holds the key

Access to higher education is the key to opening many doors for women
of color. And, Latina, Black and Asian women are increasingly well
educated. In fact, the college participation rates of women of color
relative to their male counterparts exceed those of women in general.
According to the U.S. Department of Education, over 64 percent of
all African Americans in college are women compared with 56 percent

of non-Hispanic Whites in college who are women; 59 percent of all Hispanics in college are women; 54 percent of all Asian/Pacific Islanders in college are women. Women of color out-rank the number of men of color in college by a full six percentage points. Fifty-seven percent of college students of color are women; 43 percent are men.

Where do the educational focus and clarity that women of color have come from? As Patricia Russell-McCloud shared during our interview for this book:

> "Females early on become steeped in the knowledge and understanding of what they really want and where they are really going. As they go through the seriousness of purpose it holds them hostage . . . to their benefit, of course. They have this 'Aha!' moment earlier than their male counterparts. They are serious pretty much from the onset."

This "Aha!" moment is evident in the data. The U.S. Department of Education goes on to report that 43 percent of all Asian American women over the age 25 have graduated from college compared with 24 percent of the U.S. female population over age 25. Among African Americans, there will be 200 Black female graduates for every 100 Black male graduates by 2010. At the graduate and professional level, Black women are twice as likely (16 percent) to aspire toward medical degrees than are men (8 percent). Native-born Hispanic women are nearly twice as likely as foreign-born Hispanic women to have some college education (46 percent vs. 24 percent, respectively). And, thanks to steady gains in educational attainment among Latinos, 84 percent of all U.S. born Hispanics complete high school, which is comparable to the 90 percent levels experienced among the general population. In today's tight labor market, corporations must attract enough talent and human resources to sustain their company's growth. Diverse women, and women in general, whose styles are more collaborative, represent excellent candidates for these positions.

Going forward, the advancement of diverse women in the educational system will continue to swell the numbers of highly qualified and highly motivated women entering the workforce and, ultimately lead to even higher levels of purchasing power and affluence. As Patricia Russell-McCloud says, "They (women of color) are not in school to play. Their next steps are *up, out,* and *in charge."*

White baby boomer exit opens doors for diversity

According to the Department of Labor Statistics, 33 percent of all new persons added to the workforce between 2000 and 2010 will be Latino. In fact, given the growth of the diverse markets, it can be argued that the majority of all new hires joining the workforce will be well-trained persons of Hispanic, African, Asian, or Native American descent. They will close the talent gap that will be created by the mass exodus of non-Hispanic White baby boomers that have begun to retire. Companies can leverage this change in workforce structure to their benefit by proactively identifying, hiring, and training diverse candidates as members of their independent sales force, wholesale teams, and employee management groups. And since research and experience shows that consumers are more willing to buy from individuals who speak their language, understand their culture, and can empathize with their needs, there is a benefit to the bottom line in hiring more diverse talent. A diverse workforce will close talent gaps and improve your odds of success in marketing and selling to diverse customers.

Here are some important facts as reported in *DiversityInc. Best Practices* on diversity and the workplace:

- Of all women of color, Asian women have the highest level of managerial-professional attainment at 37 percent, as measured by their titles. This is comparable to Caucasian women at 36.9 percent. Twenty-six percent of African-American women and 22 percent of Latinas, respectively, held similar titles.
- Slightly over 1 percent of corporate officers in Fortune 500 companies are African-American women, translating to approximately 150 women. (Source: Catalyst)
- In 2003, 25 of the 14,000 Fortune 500 corporate officers were Latinas. (Source: Catalyst)

- In 2002, 30 of the 10,092 corporate officers in Fortune 500 companies were Asian women. (Source: Catalyst)

▶ Figure 2.13 Women and men in managerial or professional positions by ethnicity

Ethnicity/Culture	Women	Men
Caucasian/Non-Hispanic White	36.9%	33.4%
Asian American	37.2	41.0
African American	26.0	17.0
Latino/Hispanic	21.7	13.8

Source: DiversityInc., U.S. Census Bureau, 2002

Entrepreneurship and micro entrepreneurship as the new Underground Railroad

In times past, you could be guaranteed a secure retirement if you stayed long enough with a corporation. Women of color, like others, looked to companies to anchor their futures. Corporations and government jobs became their caretakers. However, times have changed and women of color, like so many others, have replaced loyalty to one company with loyalty to themselves in the form of micro enterprise. They are taking control of their destinies by starting their own businesses, managing their own security, and taking on risk. They have broadened their experience by controlling the number of clients accepted, deciding how much will be generated, and determining where and when resources will be saved or invested in the company. Entrepreneurship provides a level of freedom to women of color that enables them to leverage talents, networks, and pent-up determination to succeed, at whatever the cost.

According to The Center for Women's Business Research, there are 2.4 million businesses that are 50 percent or more owned by women of color, representing 42 percent of all businesses owned by persons of color, up from 36 percent in 2004. They generated gross sales of $230 billion and employed 1.6 million persons. This figure is slightly ahead of the ownership levels among women overall, where 41 percent of all businesses are majority owned by women, regardless of ethnicity. Between

1997 and 2006 the number of privately held firms with majority ownership by women of color grew almost six times faster than all privately
held firms (120 percent vs. 24 percent). Entrepreneurship represents
the modern "underground railroad" used by women of color to make
significant, below the radar, stealth advances to the world of major
enterprise. Women-of-color business owners are an important segment
of the diversity market that offers potential as a supplier base, marketing
partner, and customer lead for many corporations.

Another powerful form of micro enterprise, which has fueled the
economic growth of women of color, is direct selling. According to
Ms. Dyan Lucero, recently retired President of JAFRA Cosmetics U.S.
Sales, "As independent distributors, a woman has the dream of what
she can do for herself and for her family, and how she can help others
get it for themselves. That fuels the dream. If you are just doing the
work, it really is just work. It's wonderful when you have the dream and
mission to drive you. For JAFRA, and most companies, the question is
what does it [the company] stand for. The products are secondary. The
income has to be good, but the driver is the 'why.' The 'why' is bigger
than the 'how to.' You figure out the 'how to.' The 'why' is the glue
that will carry you through."

Myths on Marketing to Women of Color: Agree or Disagree?

1. When you reach women you automatically reach women of color.
2. Women of color are not as economically viable as Caucasian women.
3. You are already reaching women of color through your multicultural marketing efforts.
4. Budgets are limited. Don't split hairs with "segment within a segment"
marketing.
5. Average education and affluence among women of color is lower than it
is among Caucasian women. It's better to focus on the majority market.

What companies do not understand

Despite demographic changes, women of color have remained on the

fringes, rarely receiving the focus, attention, and understanding war-
ranted by their numbers, intelligence, influence, and affluence. In con-
ducting research for this book, I had the opportunity to ask several
distinguished leaders questions about what companies do **not** understand about women of color. Among the thought leaders I spoke with
is Ms. Joyce Roché, President of Girls, Inc.:

> "I think where companies get it, they get it in terms of the size of this
> population, and with the Latina population growth. The recognition
> that this is a large and a growing market is driven by Latinas, although
> there is growth among Asians and African Americans. The challenge
> under that umbrella is that companies sometimes think it's too simple.
> They may say, 'We are going to go after the African American market
> this time period . . . now are looking at Latinas in this time period
> . . . *those populations don't go away when the companies decide to change
> strategy.* If these audiences are a focus and are growing, that growth
> does not stop because the companies have decided to refocus else-
> where. It is simplistic to think that we can now move from the ethnic
> markets to another segment. That disenfranchises the ethnic markets.
> So, what I like about the concept of "women of color" is that it is an
> incredibly large population. Companies need to think broadly, and
> then think laser-like. Companies should not 'turn the page' or practice
> 'flavor of the month' when it comes to women of color."

Ms. Patricia Russell-McCloud, former President of The Links, Inc.,
told me:

> "Women of color are not seeking celebration; they want recognition
> on an even bar of evaluation of their abilities, expertise and interests.
> They want understanding of their competencies . . . and women of
> color would welcome the business opportunity to thrive. Specifically,
> we are the comptrollers of consumerism. That point is somehow
> missed by the larger companies, unlike The 85% Niche who come
> forward and show us, with some very irrefutable data that women
> are the helm of consumerism. We have significant mortgages, we
> buy vehicles; we buy whatever we want. That's a fact. Yet there is no

reciprocity from companies. We should be recognized and understood with product that suits our needs and meets our expectations."

Delia Passi, CEO of Medelia Communications made the point most succinctly:

"A one-size-fits-all approach [with the women's market] is just wasting dollars. They [companies] may as well toss their money in a hole and bury it."

What views do you hold about women of color? Do you assume that all women are alike? Do you gloss over questions of culture and ethnicity in your women's marketing and sales plans? Does your current business plan include a comprehensive and integrated approach to reach women of color, or do you employ the "flavor of the month" approach to planning?

How much more can you contribute to your business by realizing that you are only skimming the surface when it comes to your women's market plan? When is it absolutely essential that you move from "thinking globally" in relation to the women's market to "acting locally" to the unique needs of Latina, African-American, and Asian women? What are the geographic strongholds where your mainstream women's marketing plan represents "wasted dollars" in connecting with your real audience—Black, Latina, and Asian women? Exactly when does diversity trump gender? Let's examine this question in the next chapter.

Growing The 85% Niche: Worksheet

Areas of Inquiry	Already Addressing	New & Will Incorporate	Table & Revisit Later	Priority: High /Med / Low
What role, if any, does the Women of Color (WOC) market play in the attainment of your overall business goals?				
What percentage of your market share is attributable to WOC and what have been the historical trends?				
How does the WOC market share compare by product segment?				
Where are the critical gaps (from a profitability and category penetration perspective)? Are there plans in place to close these gaps?				
Who do you view as a major competitor in the WOC market? Can you briefly comment on their strategic efforts (product portfolio, strategies, etc.)?				
Thinking about your strategic plans, what programs do you have in place for WOC? What measurement tools do you use to assess success?				
In relation to marketing budgets, what is the allocation of spending relative to WOC? (Be specific to media spending, sponsorship, interactive, local marketing, events, communications, publicity. Probe for allocation relative to segment contribution to business.)				
Do you have targeted creative resources to engage WOC? (Probe advertising creative, message/copy development, women-centric events, etc.)				
How successful has this been? (Probe metrics.)				
What forums are in place to provide cross-functional updates on the WOC market and among your team? Are these sufficient? What other internal platforms exist or can be created to maximize learning/best practices?				
Would you be willing to be a champion of the WOC marketing?				
What are your specific plans to do so?				

THREE

Where Diversity Trumps Gender

WHAT CHARACTERISTICS define women of color from a cultural point of view? When do we come together as women, disregarding cultural background, language, and traditions? When do we re-affirm our cultural roots and rally around heritage and ethnicity as our primary identity? What are some of the non-negotiable differences that we uphold as fundamental to our *essence* as women, mothers, wives, and daughters? When does diversity "trump" gender?

A brief historical view

The answer, in part, lies in history. Women of color have always maintained a collective identity and fought for civil rights, whether it was demanding equality of the races, encouraging labor laws prohibiting discrimination against field workers, providing educational access, or a host of other human rights issues. They worked both "below the radar" and more publicly to give voice to change.

One of the more public outreach efforts among women of color was to band with the early feminist movement. The late Rev. Pauli Murray, an African-American woman and Episcopal minister was one of the founders of the National Organization of Women (NOW) and co-authored NOW's Statement of Purpose. Her strong allegiance to the women's movement was an example of how Black women—the largest of all ethnic groups in the 1960s—sought to diminish ethnicity and coalesce with "like-minded women's organizations" to drive change. However, the movement was regarded with distrust; it was seen as a radical change organization focused on mainstream (mostly White) women's issues. Many women of color later distanced themselves from the movement feeling that their voices would not be heard and understood. As a consequence, despite attempts for gender to override diversity as a coalescing agent, women of color returned to operating as autonomous organizational units.

These autonomous units blossomed in large numbers beginning in the early 1970s. Global emphasis on women, stimulated by the United Nations Decade World Conferences (Mexico City, 1975, Copenhagen, 1980, and Nairobi in 1985), the end of the Vietnam War, and the on-going civil rights movement, also worked to encourage those organizing women-of-color institutions. In particular, educational institutions played an important role in elevating discussion of women and diversity by offering extensive women's studies programs at colleges and universities. Women's studies courses expanded in the 1970s and 1980s and for the first time focused on women of color issues as noted in the development of Black women's studies in the early 1980s. Colleges and universities rallied around distinctions in ethnicity, culture, and gender as important discussion and learning topics. From an educational and intellectual point of view, it was evident that diversity was capable of trumping gender.

Outside the walls of educational institutions, organizations of women of color focused on education and family rights, which remain central values, even today. The following partial chronology gives an overview of women of color institutions in this country, including their mission and focus.

Partial Chronology of Women of Color Organizations and Institutions

1960S AND EARLIER

Latina	Black	Asian	Native American/ Indigenous	Women of Color
Dolores Huerta joins Cesar Chavez as a leader of the **National Farm Worker's Association** (later UFW). Jessie Lopez de la Cruz is the first woman union organizer in the field.	**National Council of Negro Women** (NCNW) formed in 1935 to encourage networking, coalition-building, and advocating the use of collective power on issues affecting women, their families, and communities. **Jack & Jill** founded in 1938 by a group of upper-class Black women brings their children together to provide a variety of educational, social and cultural experiences. **The Links, Inc.** founded in 1946 as an organization of professional Black women bonded by friendship. **Pan Hellenic organizations**, including the Deltas and AKAs are formed as Black sororities.			

1970S

Latina	Black	Asian	Native American/ Indigenous	Women of Color
Commission Feminil Mexicana, first national Hispanic feminist organization, founded. **National Conference of Puerto Rican Women** (NCOPRW) founded.	**National Black Feminist Organization** formed. **Combahee River Collective Statement** issued, definitive Black feminist statement combining anti-sexist, anti-racist, and anti-homophobic work.	**Asian Studies Journal** publishes *Asian Women*, first issue on pan-Asian women. **Organization of Pan Asian American Women** founded, the first national public policy and leadership development consolidation of Asian American women.	**Native American Women's Action Corps** and **North American Indian Women's Association** founded. First **International Conference of Indigenous Women of the Americas** held in Chiapas, Mexico. First **Native American Women's Studies** course, at Dartmouth College **Native American Women Writers Conference**, in Arizona.	First **Women of Color ERA** organization. First **Minority Women's Committee** within the National Organization for Women is formed.

1970S *continued*

Latina	Black	Asian	Native American/Indigenous	Women of Color
Mexican American Women National Association organizes around feminist principles. First **Hispanic Women's Center** established in New York City. **National Association of Cuban-American Women** formed.	**Black Women's Agenda** organized in Washington, D.C.,, presents proposal at National Women's Conference. **Caribbean Cultural Center** (CCC) founded to raise focus on the global African Diaspora.	**Organization of Chinese American Women** founded, first national organization for women of Chinese descent.	**National Institute of Education** sponsors a conference on Native American Women, in New Mexico. **Women of All Red Nations** (WARN) founded. **North American Indian Women's Association** is founded.	First national conference on **Third World Women and Violence Against Women** meets in Washington, D.C. Over one thousand colleges and universities offer women's studies courses and eighty have full programs.

1980S

Latina	Black	Asian	Native American/Indigenous	Women of Color
National Hispana Leadership Institute ensures the leadership and development of Latina women, providing access and power to influence public policy.	**National Coalition of 100 Black Women** founded. **International Council of African Women** founded, with international focus. **National Black Women's Health Project** begins organizing, holds conference in Atlanta in 1983, attracting over 2000 participants, the largest gathering of women of color held during that time period. **National Political Congress of Black Women** founded by Black women disappointed in the Democratic and Republican party's dismissal of Black women as a political force. First **Black Women's Political Action Committee** formed to raise funds for Black women candidates.			**National Institute for Women of Color** founded, the first national organization devoted to bringing together all women of color in a research and public policy organization. **Third World/Women of Color Caucus** organized at the National Coalition Against Domestic Violence. First **National Conference on Women of Color and Reproductive Rights**, sponsored by NOW, but organized by women of color, held in Washington, D.C. The **UN Third World Conference on Women** is held in Nairobi, Kenya.

		1990s		
Latina	**Black**	**Asian**	**Native American/ Indigenous**	**Women of Color**
MANA, a national Latina organization is launched with the goal of raising awareness on the accomplishments of Latinas, while raising funds to support educational programs for Latinas, mentor girls aged 11-17 and advocate on issues of health, education and economic well-being of Latinas. **Hispanic 100 Women** was founded in 1996 as a forum for Latinas, individuals, and organizations who support Hispanics to come together to address issues, influence policy, and promote diversity.		**Asian Women in Business** (AWIB) is a non-profit membership organization which assists Asian women entrepreneurs by providing training, information, and networking opportunities. **Philippine Nurses Association of America** (PNAA) is a national organization whose purpose is to uphold the image and foster the welfare of Philippine nurses in the U.S.		Fourth **World Conference on Women** opens in Beijing, China.

		2000s		
Madrinas is founded—an organization of Latina executives empowering other Latina executives in corporate America for professional advancement and growth.		The **Asian Pacific American Women's Leadership Institute** (APAWLI) is the only national, non-profit organization dedicated to enhancing and enriching leadership skills for Asian American and Pacific Island women leaders. The **Filipina Women's Network** (FWN) provides educational resources through publications, lectures, activities and programs to further the professional and personal development of its members.		**Women's Intercultural Exchange** (WIE) founded to build social trust among women of color in the workplace.

2000S *continued*				
Latina	**Black**	**Asian**	**Native American/ Indigenous**	**Women of Color**
		Founded in 2003, **South Asian Women's Leadership Forum** (SAWLF) is committed to providing women entrepreneurs and professionals a forum in which to interact and learn from successful business and community leaders.		

Sources: "Minority Women," in Susanna Downie, *Decade of Achievement: 1977–1987:* A Report on a Survey Based on the National Plan of Action for Women. Chicago Women's Liberation Union. www.cwluherstory.com/

A comparison of Latina, Black, and Asian women's values and American mainstream values

So what are the major cultural and "non-negotiable" differences between mainstream (White) women and women of color? The following chart summarizes these differences. These views are not intended to apply to every woman who claims Hispanic, African, Asian, or European ancestry. It is intended to give a "global view" of the major similarities and dissimilarities among women of color from a values perspective. In so doing we are able to identify the major characteristics that typically describe women of a specific cultural group. It will be valuable for brand teams to understand and leverage these basic differences into strategic business plans as the "women's market" is more clearly defined.

Mainstream Values	LATINA VALUES
Communication	
Much importance placed on social skills; networking	Warm, open, spontaneous communication style
Direct communication acceptable	Direct, engaging conversation sought, even with strangers
More physically reserved in communication	Overt emotional display acceptable; high touch
Planner; adheres to schedules	Less concerned with time/deadlines
Comfortable in expressing disagreement	Preference not to disagree in public; cordiality is important

Mainstream Values	LATINA VALUES
Can accept delayed gratification	Prefers immediate gratification
Ego vs. Others	
Self-promotion is acceptable	Focus is largely on family and community
Individuality	Collective power; low Individual visibility
Power is perceived as individual power	Power is perceived as group power
Self-determination; optimists	Religious; largely Roman Catholic: fatalistic (*Si Dios Quiere*)
Leadership	
Ability to push the envelope with parents and authority figures	Respect for authority figures; doctors/parents not questioned
No fear of opposing authority	Fear of opposing authority
Independence	Inter-dependence; team
Individual leadership, responsibility & ownership	Team accountability
Democratic view of rights for all	Belief in hierarchy and social class
American Dream	
Owning a home viewed as a "given"	Home ownership part of the American dream
College education viewed as a "given" for children	College education part of the American dream
Personal possessions important	Well-known brands a sign of success
Retirement restaged as re-engagement with life	Niche segments of affluent prepared for retirement; majority living for present
Women have significant decision-making role	Younger women are more equally involved in decisions Older, unacculturated women less direct decisions

Mainstream Values	AFRICAN-AMERICAN VALUES
Communication	
High importance placed on social skills; networking	Guarded openness to networking; respect is key
Direct communication acceptable	Direct communication style; honest & open dialog
More physically reserved in communication	Physical display of affection limited to family/friends
Planner; adheres to schedules	Less concerned with time/deadlines
Comfortable in expressing disagreement	Comfortable in expressing disagreement
Can accept delayed gratification	Prefers immediate gratification
Ego vs. Others	
Self-promotion is acceptable	Self-promotion is acceptable
Individuality	Individuality
Power is perceived as individual power	Power is perceived as individual power

Mainstream Values	AFRICAN-AMERICAN VALUES
Self-determination; optimists	Strong belief system; spiritual
Leadership	
Ability to push the envelope with parents & authority	Distrustful relationship with authority
No fear of opposing authority	Fear of opposing authority
Independence	Independence
Individual leadership, responsibility & ownership	Individual leadership/team engagement
Democratic view of rights for all	Democratic view of rights for all
American Dream	
Owning a home viewed as a "given"	Home ownership represents retirement security
College education viewed as a "given" for children	College education as the equalizer
Personal possessions important	Prestige brands a badge of attainment & wealth
Retirement restaged as re-engagement with life	Recognition of importance of retirement; home equity and entrepreneurship key avenues for added wealth
Women have significant decision-making role	Women have significant decision-making role

Mainstream Values	ASIAN AMERICAN VALUES
Communication	
High importance placed on social skills; networking	Friendly, but controlled emotional display
Direct communication acceptable	Direct eye contact acceptable; honest open dialog
More physically reserved in communication	Hide/refrain from emotions; reserved for family/friends
Planner; adheres to schedules	Planner; adheres to schedules
Comfortable in expressing disagreement	Rarely disagree in public; prefer to be vague vs. negative
Can accept delayed gratification	Can accept delayed gratification
Ego vs. Others	
Self-promotion is acceptable	Focus on family, community, and team
Individuality	Collective power; low individual visibility
Power is perceived as individual power	Power is perceived as group power
Self-determination; optimists	Seek harmony; balance
Leadership	
Ability to push the envelope with parents & authority	Respect for authority figures; obedience & filial trust
No fear of opposing authority	Fear of opposing authority
Independence	Interdependence; team
Individual leadership, responsibility & ownership	Team accountability & ownership

Mainstream Values	ASIAN AMERICAN VALUES
Democratic view of rights for all	Belief in hierarchy and social class
American Dream	
Owning a home viewed as a "given"	Owning a home seen as essential
College education viewed as a "given" for children	High degree of importance on college/post graduate education
Personal possessions important	Strong preference for prestige & quality brands
Retirement restaged as re-engagement with life	High involvement in early planning for retirement
Women have significant decision-making role	Younger women are more equally involved in decisions
	Older, unacculturated women less direct decisions

Hips, lips, and more

Other more obvious examples of how diversity can "trump" or take precedence over gender are in relation to beauty, personal care, and fashion. Ethnicity and physiology directly affect women's purchase decisions in these industries. Women of color are disproportionate users of hair care, cosmetics, fragrance, skin care, and apparel, and therefore, represent high-profit customers. Yet many of the images seen in advertising for these product categories miss the mark in creating relevance with women of color. And, while improving, there are cosmetic product lines that still have gaps in shades and tones that are appropriate for women of color. Rather than celebrating the deep skin tones, ample, full, and generous shapes of women of color, Madison Avenue and Hollywood have the tendency to shy away from darker-skinned women with broad features, to stereotype Latinas as fair-skinned Latinas only, and to portray "thin" as the gold standard for all. And, few Asian-American women are portrayed in advertising communications. Women of color see through these feigned attempts at relevance and generally regard them as a turn off.

Owing primarily to the popularity of beautiful Black and Latina "mega-stars," there seems to be a greater acceptance of women who are well endowed and have unique, distinctive beauty features. The voluptuous, ample bodies of many Black and Latina women are beginning to move into the mainstream of American beauty standards. The full shapes of well-known actresses such as Grammy-winner Beyoncé Knowles, Oscar-winning Jennifer Hudson, Cover Girl spokesperson and actress Queen Latifah, *Sports Illustrated* model and talk-show/reality TV host Tyra Banks, singer-actress-dancer Jennifer López, Mexican singer Selena, Chandra Wilson of *Grey's Anatomy*, and Sara Ramirez are all examples of well-endowed women of color who made their personal beauty the new standard among women in general. Going back further in time, we have singers such as Charo, Iris Chacón, Patti LaBelle, Chaka Khan, and Célia Cruz—all full-figured women of color who turned heads with their ample curves. And, while Asian women tend to have smaller and more delicate body frames there are some exceptions, as noted by the rising popularity of Korean comedian-turned-actress, Margaret Cho. The bottom line is that women of color are proud of their deep skin tones, full lips, generous hips, and ample breasts. These are non-negotiable physical differences that have become part of the cultural persona. Marketing should reflect these true images in their advertising campaigns.

Women of color are also more accepting of the *power* of their womanliness and of the intuitive energy that is embodied in the feminine. Studies by *Essence Magazine* and *People en Español* report that women of color have higher levels of body confidence than their Caucasian counterparts. When Shakira, the famous Argentinean and Armenian singer, made popular the song, "Hips Don't Lie," she was singing more than just words to a love song. She was speaking about sensuality as a woman of color. She was saying that, above all things, she could trust her femininity, her intuitive senses, and her "womanliness" in judging a situation as right or wrong for her.

"And I'm on tonight
You know my hips don't lie
And I'm starting to feel it's right
All the attraction, the tension
Don't you see baby, this is perfection"

Source: www.moron.nl/lyrics

Failed beauty images

Where do companies fail in understanding the beauty images of women of color? What is it that they just don't get? According to Deborah Gray-Young, media and advertising executive, the answer is related to the concept of "worthiness."

> "[Companies] underestimate that people like to see themselves and so I may be a woman but to assume that Nicole Kidman and her standard of beauty is my beauty (and don't get me wrong, she is a beautiful woman) is just wrong. They underestimate that women of color are worthy of being spoken to or invited, that we have the purchasing power to make a difference . . . and it may not be trillions of dollars today, but in this competitive landscape every bit helps."

Indeed, the competitive nature of today's marketplace requires that companies extend invitations to women of color that are personal and relevant. European images cannot be expected to connect on a deep level with beauty standards of women of color. Brands must clearly communicate that their products are formulated with the unique needs of women of color in mind and validate this promise using images that resonate on a personal level. That means incorporating large full-bodied women, deep skin tones, authentic true Latina, Black, and Asian women, and depicting women in situations that are real. This also means celebrating our wide range of beauty through products that address our unique needs, and with promotions that engage and draw us in. Moreover, in a day when customers have more control than ever over advertising messages, this means gaining access into the world of women of color, through targeted ethnographic research and tailored marketing studies. The important point to leverage from a practical point of view is to use a range of women's body shapes, skin tones, and facial features in advertising, in your community outreach, in your recruiting, and in your marketing research and sales programs.

Myths that lead to mishaps: Assumptions about diversity and gender

1. Affluence trumps diversity

While there is a fair amount of debate on the subject, general thinking suggests that the higher the educational and income level of women of color relative to their mainstream counterparts, the less differentiation that exists between groups. On the surface, income and education appear to neutralize differences among women of different ethnic backgrounds. However, while education gives access to new ways of thinking and clarity of thought, the feelings behind those ideas do not necessarily morph into mainstream values simply because of an Ivy-League college diploma or a six-figure salary.

Many affluent and educated women of color remain connected with their roots and traditions. However, they are able to monetize their relationship with those traditions for more creative outlet and expression. For example, a Latina or Asian female entrepreneur who has successfully built a business from ground zero may stay connected to her roots by donating time and philanthropic efforts to the neighborhood where she once lived. She has not lost her identity or her concern for collective empowerment as a woman of color; she is using her economic resources to further actualize that strong cultural value. Or, a highly educated African-American woman who enjoys African sculpture may evolve from visiting museums as her primary pastime to actually visiting West Africa or Egypt to view—and purchase—artifacts, designs, and other cultural motifs.

2. Recruiting messages trump diversity

Many business leaders and talent officers miss the power that differentiated recruiting messages have with employees of color. Not all employees and prospective candidates will react in the same way to a common corporate recruiting campaign. On the surface we are the same, but how we live and what we need to accomplish for our families on a day-to-day basis is very different. Therefore, the motivators need to be different. For example, the concept of a "flexible work environment" may be the right motivator for a Caucasian mother entering the workforce, but it is not necessarily the prime motivator for all women candidates. Here are some examples:

> Among **African Americans,** being in control of one's destiny and having self-respect and the respect of others in the community are important career motivators. Recruiting messages that reinforce the concept of building a career filled with opportunities for advancement, recognition, and reward are effective because they *inspire hope* for a positive future. That is one of the reasons for Avon Products Inc.'s early success in the African-American market. Black women in the 1950s and 1960s who could not enter a department store to try on makeup (or clothes) could enjoy a professional career as an Avon Representative selling beauty products door-to-door. They were respected in the community as professionals, and they inspired confidence and beauty in others through the many fine products sold. Direct selling became a gateway for building wealth and self-esteem among women of color and continues to do so today.

> Among **Latinas,** "family unity" and "advancing together" are important motivational messages. Knowing that one's hard work will lead to opportunities to participate in the "American Dream" is vital—particularly for immigrant, first-generation Latinas who may come to this country with less financial means. Hispanics are known for very strong work ethics, tremendous familial and extended family pride, and doing whatever it takes to succeed, even if it means working two full-time jobs, taking care of the family, and being a *madrina* [godmother] to others in the community. A flexible work arrangement is a nice luxury, but offering the opportunity to be a part of the *American Dream* resonates on a deeper level with Latinas. There is a greater willingness to sacrifice in the short term—even if it means spending less time with family. Ms. Yesenia Morillo-Gual, a financial services vice president, offered this life experience as a testimony of sacrifices made for the sake of the family:

"Sometimes we are so hungry for success that our focus unintentionally shifts. I recall in 2006, an incident with my older son Branden that forced me to take a visual step back and carefully analyze my priorities. It was during a time where my chances of a promotion were high and I was grasping opportunities for face time with the decision makers. On a Friday morning in particular, I was serving as a speaker in a conference where many of our division and firm managers would be present. I wanted to get to work extra early to prepare. With my husband on travel, I needed to get the kids up and out much earlier, rushing and brushing them off. On route to school, Branden asked if I could stay with them for a little while longer and I responded "I don't have time, I have a meeting" and he quickly asked "When am I going to be a meeting?" I promised to pick him and his brother up early and do whatever he wanted, but it broke my heart for my son to think that he wasn't as important."

Among **Asians,** themes that reinforce association with companies that have a track record of success are important. These recruiting messages provide affirmation of having made a smart decision by joining a particular company. The company's long history, recognition as a leader, high quality products, brand equity, and strong financial performance provide important re-affirmation that should be incorporated in corporate recruiting campaigns.

3. Technology trumps diversity

New media such as blogs and online communities are increasingly a part of public relations and other marketing programs. They are also increasingly important to women of color and, when leveraged from a cultural point of view, can represent a powerful medium to reach diverse women. We know that acculturation, language, and education play a role in Hispanic Internet use, with a higher degree of involvement among U.S.-born Hispanics and lower involvement among Spanish-dominant Hispanics, although this segment is growing. Hispanic Internet users are visiting niche Spanish-language publishers to get more in depth content in their particular area of interest, from finance and fashion to sports and technology. African-American women are more involved in web technology than their male counterparts (60 percent vs. 50 percent, respectively). Asians have the highest degree of Internet use, exceeding that of the population overall. Therefore, the new technology has penetrated fairly well among diverse audiences of women.

Women's desires to network, form bonds, and continuously learn make "new technology," such as blogs and online communities, a medium of choice. However, the content must be relevant for maximum relevance. Using broadcast and print media as the benchmark, it's been proven that reach does not necessarily always guarantee relevant exposure. African-American households in the U.S. watch more television in Primetime, Daytime, and Late Night on average than all other U.S. homes across all age groups. In addition, African Americans are heavy users of Black-targeted programming delivered by cable and in print. However, African-American media use is enhanced when the right advertising creative, using culturally relevant themes, casting, and lifestyle situations is used to connect with the market. And of course, language—in addition to the right cultural cues—is key in reaching Spanish and Asian language dominant segments of the women's market.

My experience is that women of color are not "provider loyal," but are "content loyal." Brands that think through ways to integrate diversity and gender savvy content into their messages and on their sites will be rewarded with returning women of color customers, again and again.

PART TWO

Leading Voices—
A Closer Look at
Our Women

FOUR

Latina Leading Voices

THE NEARLY 22 MILLION "voices" of Latinas in the U.S. represent a vibrant, dynamic, and *essential* audience of thriving consumers, budding, and successful entrepreneurs, and talented employees for corporations across America. There is no better time than *now* to take a critical look at the business model you've relied on for growth in the general market and determine what, if any, value it still holds for you in reaching this multi-billion dollar segment. Even if you have a business plan in place to reach Latinas, you may not want to get too comfortable with it, because the market is moving at warp speed and a "change mindset" is essential for success. Strategies that were effective in reaching the Hispanic market of the past have little relevance to the Latina of today. Latinas of all geographic origins are changing the way companies must do business to remain competitive.

The population of Latinas is large and *complex*. The U.S. Census Bureau accelerated the date by which the minority markets will become the *majority* markets in the U.S.—from 2050 to 2042. This is due in large part to the exponential growth of the Hispanic population, which will *triple* in size to 133 million within just four decades. The Latina segment of this population includes foreign born, U.S. born, acculturated, retro-acculturated, un-acculturated, Spanish dominant, English dominant, bi-lingual, Mexicans, Cubans, Puerto Ricans, Dominicans, Central Americans, Latin Americans and those from Spain. And, they are racially mixed, with Caucasian, Indian, and African blood (and in some Caribbean islands Asians are a factor), so there is no one "physical look" to represent the broad spectrum of Latinas (and Latinos) globally and in the United States.

Attitudinally, Latinas are determined, very committed to the long-term, and extremely dedicated to doing all they can for the benefit of their families and communities—even at the expense of their personal comfort and needs. They are the *madrinas*—the godmothers and caretakers of those in need and the selfless and tireless givers of love, support, and encouragement. This support and love can come in the form of an open home and place to stay if one is without residence. It can come in the form of a delicious meal of *arroz, habichuelas, pollo guisado, y tostones*—even if there is very little food in the home. "*Siempre hay comida para la familia*," my parents would say to unexpected guests at dinnertime. "*Si uno come, todos comen*" . . . if one eats, we all eat. It's amazing to me how my mother was able to stretch her dollars to make enough food to feed an army if necessary! And, of course, it was always deliciously prepared, "*con mucho amor y cariño*." This is the soul of the Latina woman.

La mujer Latina's boundless commitment to family is matched by her determination to succeed and her relentless pursuit of survival. "*Hay que adelantar la raza*" . . . or, "one must advance the race/group," is a constant motivation urging Latinas onward. Educational attainment, as we will see in this chapter, is on the rise, as are solid entrepreneurial gains for Latina majority owned businesses. So as a business leader you will want to *remain vigilant* and *stay on your toes* as you give serious thought to the strategic changes in your plans that are required to get your fair share of this highly attractive consumer market.

¿Pero, Quién Es La Mujer Latina?

Who is this woman? What are some of the important demographic, economic, and cultural nuances of women of Hispanic ancestry? Read on to learn more.

Latina "Leading Voices" niche snapshot

There is no question that Latina women are the dominant female ethnic group in this country. There are 22 million females of Hispanic ancestry living in the U.S., a number that has grown by 28.2 percent since

2000. This is four times faster than the growth of women overall, who increased 6.7 percent during this same time period.

▶ Figure 4.1   Population growth among women

U.S. females	2007	2000	% Growth
Latina	21,980,731	17,144,023	28.2%
Black	21,286,017	19,461,176	9.4
Asian American	8,291,405	6,623,231	25.2
Asian	*7,784,432*	*6,172,636*	*26.1*
Native Hawaiian/Pacific Islander	*506,973*	*450,595*	*12.5*
American Indian/Native Alaskan	2,292,162	2,136,916	7.3
Total women of color (Includes all females of color in the U.S.)	53,850,315	45,365,346	18.7
Total U.S. females	152,962,259	143,368,343	6.7

Source: U.S. Census Bureau

Spanish remains language preference

Approximately 75 to 80 percent of U.S. Hispanic adults speak Spanish at home, of which one-third treat English as their second language. Thirty-five percent of U.S. born Hispanics speak English well; only 4 percent of foreign-born Hispanics speak English well. Spanish clearly remains the dominant language of choice and the first language taught by parents. Ninety-four percent of U.S. born Hispanics learn to speak Spanish before they learn English and that language is most often taught by the mother. In addition to the role of the Latina mother in reinforcing the language's use at home, Spanish remains the U.S. Hispanic market's language of choice for several other reasons, including the geographic clustering of the market, which makes it easier to interact without having to speak English, continued immigration as a source of Hispanic population growth, the proliferation of Spanish-language media, and the importance of the language as a way to self-identify with the Hispanic culture. As proof of this last point, 90 percent of Latinas rate language as the one aspect of the culture that must be maintained among their children. Figure 4.2 shows the English-speaking ability of Hispanic *women*.

▶ **Figure 4.2   English-speaking ability of adult Hispanic women, by nativity, 2006**

	English only	English very well	English less than very well
Hispanic	19%	37%	45%
U.S. born	35	51	14
Foreign born	4	23	73

Note: Data based on survey response. Percentages may not add to 100 due to rounding.

Source: Pew Hispanic Center tabulations of the 2006 American Community Survey

Latina youthfulness of age and implications

Hispanic women are much younger than their general market coun-terparts as evidenced in the age cohort analysis of women of color and women overall (Figure 4.3) The data from the U.S. Census shows that Latinas are the youngest of all women of color, with a median age of 27.8 years. They are an average of 3.4 years younger than other women of color and 14.3 years younger than non-Hispanic white females in this country. Hispanic women born in the U.S., who represent 48 percent of all U.S. Latinas, tend to be younger than their foreign-born counterparts by an average of three years. This makes them attractive for youth-oriented products (technology, music, beauty, fashion, digital communication).

Companies whose target market is comprised primarily of women aged 18 to 44 will want to pay particular attention to Latinas because they dominate this age cohort. A full 42 percent of all Hispanic women are aged 18 to 44 compared with 34 percent of non-Hispanic White women. We know from experience that people in this age group are most responsive to brand messages and are primary purchasers across many categories.

At the other extreme of the age spectrum, there are fewer Latinas approaching retirement age than any other multicultural segment. Only 6.5 percent of Latinas are aged 65 and over, compared with 17.4 percent of non-Hispanic White women. Retirement planning, elder care, age-related pharmaceutical products, and life insurance services are impor-tant opportunity segments for the Hispanic market. In general, Latinas tend to be more focused on the immediate, short term, versus having a long-term perspective. Although the demographics indicate there are fewer Latinas in the older population groups experiencing the need for these services, nonetheless, companies would be wise to plan now for the future realities as Latinas age.

LATINA LEADING VOICES INTERVIEW

On the "Voice" of the Latina Woman—Needs, Aspirations, and Values

From my perspective, the voice of the Latina woman is a person who is empowered both in work and at home but for whom family is a priority, and so she builds her world around that. From my perspective, I chose not to have a job that would relocate me; I chose to stay in one place and perhaps that affected certain career moves through the years but it was the choice that I made for the sake of my family. And I think that a lot of Latina women share that perspective.

As a Latina and member of the powerful **85% Niche,** I represent a strong buying power and a strong influence. I buy for my family; I don't necessarily buy clothing for myself but my children get new wardrobes every year. I want companies to know that I have a lot of spending power and it's not just in "fluff." I buy real estate, I buy land, and I make investments. I also buy vehicles, but I do those with other people in mind. I'll get in the back seat and make sure that it's comfortable, roomy and safe—as safe as the front seats are because that's where my children sit. I also will be looking at things that are needed for the community and the work that I do there. I may be on the board of directors and I may also be on the little league. So, I have a lot of needs that need to be met and I need those to be met efficiently and with the minimum amount of time and, no haggle. I know what I want and I want to be met half way with those needs.

Such planning will require a re-education among Latinas of the need to take care of themselves *first*—a concept understood and increasingly embraced by non-Hispanic White women. Because women outlive men by an average of seven years and due to cultural values that place an emphasis on "others" versus the "self," many older Latina widows rely on other family members to care for them as they age. This has a tremendous impact on the need for a sound financial strategy. As Latinas earn on average 52 cents for every dollar that non-Hispanic White men earn, their wealth and financial resources have to work harder and longer than men's do. In addition, because the Latino household is largely a patriarchal society, although Latina women still *influence* the majority of all purchase decisions, women are often unprepared for the financial challenges presented by the more-than-likely loss of a spouse.

Further, there is a cultural stigma associated with mainstream American elder care choices. Except in extreme cases, the idea of putting one's parent into a nursing home is almost unheard of in the Latino community. It is less about the quality of the services offered in the nursing home than it is about the broader generalization that no environment can match the love and care one receives from *familia*. Therefore, successfully positioning your product or service against the future generation of older Latinas will require a re-education of self-value and worth to *today's* Latinas, as well as an evaluation of how your products can be more closely aligned with the cultural values of the Latino community.

Age and workforce opportunities

The group aged 18-to-44 also represents significant value as prospective employees and emerging talent. As noted in an earlier chapter, 33 percent of all new persons added to the workforce between 2000 and 2010 will be Latino. They will close the talent gap that will be created by the mass exit of baby boomers beginning to retire over the next 20 years. Companies can leverage this change in workforce structure to their benefit by proactively identifying, hiring, and training diverse candidates as members of their independent sales forces, wholesale teams, and employee management groups. Consumers are more willing to buy from individuals who speak their language, understand their culture, and look like them. Therefore, integrated business plans—including marketing, sales, and talent-recruiting plans—should be adjusted accordingly to invite Latinas to experience both the brand *and* the company's career opportunities.

▶ Figure 4.3   Latinas and women of color by age segment, 2007

	Hispanic	Women of color	Non-Hisp. White
Females	21,980,731	53,850,315	101,346,238
Under 18 years	**34.3%**	**30.4%**	**20.2%**
Under 5 years	10.9	9.1	5.4
5 to 13 years	16.5	14.6	9.9
14 to 17 years	6.9	6.7	4.9
18 to 64 years	**59.2%**	**61.4%**	**62.4%**
18 to 24 years	10.9	10.7	8.7
25 to 44 years	31.3	30.4	25.4
45 to 64 years	17.0	20.3	28.3
65 years and over	**6.5%**	**8.2%**	**17.4%**
Median age (years)	27.8	31.2	42.1

Source: U.S. Census Bureau

THINK ABOUT IT

U.S. Hispanic Women are the largest ethnic women's group in this country. How does this affect your decisions about:

Your Mainstream Women's Marketing Plan

What enhancements to your current women's marketing strategy are essential to ensure you are connecting with the 22 million Latinas in this country? What assumptions are you making about women that do not include the voices and needs of these 22 million potential customers?

Your Communication Message

Do you incorporate Spanish-language content and culturally relevant platforms to reach Latina women? Do you understand how to reach the bi-lingual Hispanic market within your mainstream communication strategy?

Your Sales Expectations

Do you have a specific sales target in mind when focusing on Latina customers? Do you have the internal infrastructure and database models to retrieve gender and ethnicity sales? If so, how well are you performing to expectation? What changes are needed to stay ahead of the growth curve of the Latina market?   *continues . . .*

> **Your Workforce**
> Are you working to create a workforce that mirrors the Latina customer market? What plans do you have in place to recruit more Latinas into your workforce?

Increasingly well educated

Latinas are making steady gains in closing the learning gap and enjoying the access provided by higher education. U.S.-born Latinas are leading the way. Specifically, second and third generation Latinas are nearly twice as likely as those foreign-born to have some college education. A full 47 percent of native-born Latinas have some years of higher education compared with 24 percent of those who are immigrants. Fifty-eight percent of non-Hispanic women have comparable college completion levels. Latinas from South America and the Caribbean have the highest rates of college participation at 82 percent and 71 percent, respectively. And, 60 percent of all post-graduate Latino students are women.

► Figure 4.4   Educational attainment of women, 2007

	Less than high school	High school grad	Some college	College grad
Non-Hispanic	10%	32%	30%	28%
Hispanic	36	29	22	12
U.S.-born Hispanic	22	31	32	15
Foreign-born Hispanic	49	28	14	10

Note: Percentages may not total 100 due to rounding

Source: Pew Hispanic Center tabulations of the 2007 Current Population Survey

Economic picture: money and affluence

Money

Buying power among Hispanics continues to climb to record numbers, and Latinas are making sure they get their fair share of the growing pie. In 2000, Hispanics accounted for $550 billion in buying power; by 2005 that number swelled to $735.6 billion, and by 2010 the buying power of Latinos will rise to $1.1 trillion. This makes the U.S. Hispanic market the largest Latin American economy in the world, an economy that is available and accessible, right here in our own backyard.

Latinas are making powerful strides in generating income and creating wealth among all Hispanics. Due in part to successes in educational achievement, growth in professional ranks, entrepreneurship, and immigration of wealthy Latin American families emigrating to the U.S. from Venezuela and Columbia, the financial impact Latinas have in the market place is steadily growing. In 2007, based on Hispanic buying power of $860 billion, Latina women generated approximately one-third, or $284 billion. Latina women will have an estimated $330 billion in buying power by 2010. Cubans and Central/South Americans command the highest median household income as shown below.

▶ Figure 4.5   Hispanic median household income by country of origin

	Median household income
All U.S. Hispanics	$33,100
Mexico	$32,000
Central/South America	$39,000
Puerto Rico	$30,300
Cuba	$40,760
U.S. median, all households	$42.409

Source: U.S. Census Bureau

Affluence

There are certain geographic markets where upscale Latino families—those earning $200,000 plus—are more likely to live. These markets are Los Angeles, New York, Miami, San Francisco, Houston, Chicago, Dallas, Riverside/San Bernardino, San Jose, and Washington, D.C. Together, these ten metro markets account for 49 percent of all Latino households with a woman present and whose income is in excess of $200,000 per year. The combined total annual gross income of these markets is well over 10 billion dollars. If your products are upscale in nature or if you seek to drive brand consideration among an influential segment of Latinas, these are the geographic strongholds where you will want to concentrate resources and planning efforts.

▶ **Figure 4.6   Metro areas where most affluent Hispanics are found**

number of Hispanic households with incomes above $200,000

Los Angeles	12,588
New York	10,752
Miami	9,685
San Francisco	3,366
Houston	3,339
Chicago	3,288
Dallas	2,203
Riverside/San Bernardino	2,197
San Jose	2,056
Washington, D.C.	2,048
Total	51,524

Source: U.S. Census Bureau, 2004

What we buy

In aggregate, the spending power of Latinas is spread across several categories. Latinas influence the purchase decision of many products at least at the level of women in general, and in some cases higher. In the automotive industry, women's new vehicle registrations represent 45 percent of all new vehicle registrations. This is comparable to new vehicle purchases among Hispanic women. However, in the beauty products industry, Latinas over index versus the general market across all segments (eye makeup, blush, lipstick, nail care, skin care, fragrance, shampoo, conditioner). They shop more often, and according to a study by *People en Español,* 50 percent of Latinas agree that they like to use brands that demonstrate they have "made it" in America. Brands are a sign of affirmation and validation of success. It's no surprise that according to *Advertising Age,* marketers spent an estimated $5 billion in 2005 to create strong brand impressions in reaching the Hispanic market.

The following chart demonstrates where Hispanic households spend their income on a median basis. It is based on the Selig Center *Economic Report* and extrapolated to U.S. Census population and household figures.

▶ Figure 4.7   Aggregate median spending of Hispanic households by category, 2005 and 2010 projected

Category	2005 (in millions)	2010 projected (in millions)
Food at home	$50,700	$59,300
Food away from home	$29,700	$34,800
Alcoholic beverages	$4,400	$5,100
Housing	$173,500	$203,100
Apparel & services	$24,900	$29,100
Transportation	$95,600	$111,800
Health care	$20,500	$24,000
Entertainment	$17,600	$20,500
Personal care	$6,800	$8,000
Reading	$500	$600
Education	$6,800	$8,000
Tobacco products	$2,400	$2,900
Cash contribution	$8,300	$9,700
Personal insurance	$40,000	$46,800
Miscellaneous	$5,900	$6,800
All combined	$487,600	$570,500

Source: Based on Selig Center Median HH Expenditures and U.S. Census HH Projections

Geography—top ten markets

Geographically, the Latina population is concentrated in the top ten markets of: Los Angeles (18 percent total U.S.), New York (10 percent), Miami (4 percent), Chicago (4 percent), Houston (4 percent), Dallas (3 percent), San Francisco (3 percent), San Antonio (3 percent), Phoenix (3 percent), and Rio Grande (2 percent). Combined, these markets account for 54 percent of the entire U.S. Latina market. The majority of those in these markets are foreign-born with a preference for Spanish language. If you are doing business in any of these markets, you have a huge opportunity to grow sales by focusing on Hispanics in several ways: as customers of your products, as independent distributors, as suppliers for your business, and as employees of your company. Using a bilingual and Spanish language communication strategy, concentrating budgets in these top Latina markets, and using a local market approach will generate incremental sales in a measurable and targeted way.

▶ Figure 4.8   Top ten markets for Latinas

	% of total U.S. Hispanic population	Latina population in 000s	% U.S. born	% Foreign born
Los Angeles	18%	3,956	28%	72%
New York	10	2,198	24	76
Miami	4	879	13	87
Chicago	4	879	23	77
Houston	4	879	30	70
Dallas	3	659	30	70
San Antonio	3	659	28	72
San Francisco	3	659	67	33
Phoenix	3	659	37	63
Rio Grande Valley	2	439	44	56
Total	54%	11,866	29%	71%

Source: U.S. Census Bureau

Country of origin and cultural heritage

Understanding culture and its importance to Latinas is key in establishing connectivity with the market. Although Hispanic women share a great deal in common irrespective of country of origin, there are differences that marketers need to take into consideration as tactical plans are being shaped. These differences are noted in the music, foods, major holidays, and certain words in the Spanish language.

To begin, 77 percent of Hispanics now living in the U.S. come from another country. Their origins, however, cannot be neatly pigeonholed. They come from 22 different countries, with the dominant ones being Mexico, Cuba, Puerto Rico, the Dominican Republic and countries in Central/South America. Mexico remains the primary country of origin for Latinas in this country as it does for Latinos, overall. The percentages vary only slightly, with more Latinas reporting ancestry from Central and

South America than Hispanics overall. Specifically, 60 percent of Latinas report Mexican ancestry compared with 64 percent of Hispanics overall. Twenty-six percent of Latinas report Central and South American ancestry compared with 20 percent of Hispanics overall. The largest growth over the last decade has occurred among Central and South Americans, who have grown in population size by 97 percent.

▶ **Figure 4.9   Hispanic country of origin**

	Hispanics overall	Latinas	+/− Points
Mexico	64 %	60%	−4
Central America	11	14	+3
South America	9	12	+3
Caribbean	15	13	−2
Other	1	1	—
Total	100	100	—

Source: U.S. Census Bureau, PEW Hispanic Center

Geographically there are specific Hispanic groups that dominate, as shown in Figure 4.10. For example, Mexicans represent the largest Hispanic segment within Los Angeles at 64 percent. However, Caribbean Latinos from Puerto Rico, the Dominican Republic and Cuba are the dominant group in New York with over 50 percent. Again, this is an opportunity for businesses to think globally, but act "locally" before embarking on tactical plans that will resonate with Latinas. It's an opportunity to authenticate the brand experience by weaving relevant Latina traditions and customs into marketing and promotional programs.

▶ **Figure 4.10   Latina country of origin by top markets**

	Los Angeles	New York	Miami	San Francisco
Mexico	64%	9%	2%	45%
Central America	14	5	17	21
South America	2	11	6	5
Puerto Rico	1	37	4	3
Cuba	1	2	52	1
Dominican Republic	0	18	3	0
All others	18	18	16	25
Total	4,956,000	2,198,000	879,000	659,000

Note the significant differences in county of origin between the East and West coasts.

Source: U.S. Census Bureau

Customs and traditions

Family, socializing with friends, happiness, and festive events are important cornerstones in the Hispanic culture and the family, as a group, is
a high priority. As we will examine in greater detail in chapter seven,
"Mothers of Color," Latina women are disproportionately represented
among the population of mothers in this country. More specifically,
while 55 percent of all U.S. females aged 15 to 44 are mothers, *73 percent of Hispanic women, 15 to 44, are mothers.* Stated differently, Latinas
aged 15 to 44 are 32 percent more likely than women in the same age
group to be mothers. Moreover, 45 percent of Hispanics consider their
family as the primary source of their satisfaction versus 21 percent of
the mainstream consumer market. As a result, the Hispanic household
includes more children and extended family members compared with
the general market. While the Census shows at least 3.6 persons per
household among Latinas (compared with 2.6 for the mainstream market), the number is much higher if you consider grandparents, aunts,
uncles, and cousins who often live with the nuclear family.

Latinas are also very *religious* and approximately 75 percent of the
Mexican-American population, the largest of all Latino populations, is of
the Catholic faith. In the southwestern United States over two-thirds of
the Catholics are Mexican or Mexican American. The Roman Catholic
Church is also strong among other Hispanic groups, including Puerto
Ricans, Cubans, and Central Americans.

One important pastime in Hispanic families, in addition to community and social events, is watching *sports*. In the top ten markets
alone, 89 percent of the Hispanic population watches sports on television. Although viewership leans heavily toward the men in the family,
Latina women will be involved as well. Professional boxing is favored,
garnering 68 percent viewership. Major League Baseball with a 57.8
percent viewership and Major League Soccer follows closely with 53.7
percent viewership. Obviously, given these high penetration rates, tying
into sports—either as a promotional sponsor or from a media integration
perspective—is a particularly effective strategy for companies to consider
in reaching Hispanic families.

LATINA LEADING VOICES INTERVIEW

On the Importance of Family

As a Latina, I never imagined not having children because family is such an important part of our lives. Home is the center of the family so it's very important to me. I'll spend money in making (my home) beautiful and comfortable and I tend to spend money on things that foster togetherness; so, recreational vehicles, a boat, a camper, a great entertainment system with a great slew of family movies; anything that fosters that togetherness. I actually purchased a television set for each of my kid's rooms; I didn't see them for a year, so I got rid of them. And we restricted use of video games for the same reason. So, I try to make sure that what we do, we can do as a family.

Speaking on behalf of Latina women, we are very active with our families. It's not just me going with my husband to buy the house; it's bringing the family. It's not just me going to a dealership to buy a car; it's bringing the family. Unless somebody understands how we operate as a family unit, you will never really understand our potential. It's kind of funny 'cause the van opens up and the "abuelos" and "abuelas" (grandfathers and grandmothers) come out too when you're looking at a house. So, as a Latina what companies need to understand is that family is integral to everything. When we go to purchase a house, we bring the family because it's a group purchase. When we purchase a vehicle, we bring the family, for the same reasons. Everything we do is for the good for the family unit and so retailers need to understand that and meet us with those needs—whether it be larger areas for the family to look at something or just some understanding when we all get out of the car that this is the way that we're going to purchase.

Country of origin specific snapshots

For a more detailed description of the culture and background of the Latino population, you may visit *www.everyculture.com* a website with in-depth data and historical references for the U.S. Hispanic market by country of origin, including other ethnic populations.

Marriage and family

Marriage and family life are at the crux of the Latino culture, community, and socialization, and roughly half of all Hispanic women are married (51 percent compared with 52 percent of all women). More foreign-born Latinas are married (63 percent) versus U.S. born Latinas at 44 percent. As such, many traditional and primarily foreign-born Latinas are raised with the expectation that they must devote a great amount of time to nurturing the family and to creating a warm, supportive home life. Somehow they manage to squeeze in time to work full time, cook and clean, take care of their men, visit and stay in touch with family outside the U.S., and more.

▶ Figure 4.11 Latina marital status

Fifty-six percent of all U.S.-born Latinas are single; 37 percent of foreign-born Latinas are single.

Marital Status	Latina	U.S.-born Latinas	Foreign-born Latinas	Women of color	Women 15+
Married	50.9%	44%	63%	44.2%	52.2%
Divorced	8.8	15	13	10.1	10.8
Widowed	5.6	6	6	7.8	10.5
Separated	4.6	***	***	4.6	2.5
Never Married	30.1	34	18	33.5	24.0
Total Single	49.1	56	37	55.8	47.8

***Included in Divorced statistic

Source: PEW Hispanic Center

Marriage and workforce dynamics

Navigating marriage and a career can be difficult for some Latinas. Latino men—particularly older, traditional men—can be difficult, especially those who are trapped into believing the archaic view of women as subservient and that males should rule the home with an iron fist. Unfortunately, these men can present a real problem to Latinas who want to advance and make a life for themselves and for their children. There is a balance that these women who are successful in being assertive in the workplace must find in catering to the *machismo* personalities of traditional Latino men, yet at the same time asserting themselves when their needs are compromised. One Latina executive I interviewed said: "I think that has always been a struggle (work life). When I am at work, I am very American and at home I am very Latina . . . there is a shifting that takes place. You are nurturing, you are there for your family, but at work you need to (be assertive). We have to do it 200 percent. For a Latina woman, our culture is more ingrained . . . we have to do it all and take care and handle family." During another interview, a Latina who married a "gringo" shared this humorous comment: "My mother didn't approve of my extensive work-related travel. *'Tienes suerte que te casaste con un Americano porque un Latino no te hubiera dejado . . .'*" [Translation: You are lucky that you married an American man because a Latino would not have let you . . . (travel, etc.)]

Whether compromising by working harder and smarter, or finding a mate who is accepting of the cultural "pulls" on Latina women, more and more of us are finding solutions to blending traditions with present day realities. Latinas are successful in moving forward, as evidenced by the increases of those attending college, the growth of Latinas in the workplace, and the number of new Latina entrepreneurs. The younger generation of Latino couples are finding it easier to have powerful careers and to share responsibilities at home. One younger Latina thought leader shared this comment on living in two worlds: "While family is most important, sometimes you rely on your spouse to handle the children and other things . . . it's a juggle, a concerted effort to prioritize, and respect and support for each other. My husband and I have a 50/50 relationship, in that both of us can perform and are responsible for all aspects of our family lives. We do everything like a partnership. If I can cook, and do for the kids, he can, too."

LATINA LEADING VOICES INTERVIEW

On Challenges in the Workplace

As a Latina, it's time for our power—our buying power—to be recognized. My viewpoint is that if you don't reckon with us and understand us, make an effort to reach us on our terms, then you risk losing us. We have tremendous buying power and it would be something that would affect your bottom line eventually. This occurs not only at a retail level but at an employment level, as well. If you don't meet our needs both at the retail level and at the employer level then we'll find a way to do it on our own and we won't need you at some point. So, my message to corporations would be: pay attention.

"When I am at work, I am very American and at home I am very Latina . . ."

Sixty-two percent of Latinas who are married and have children under age 18 are in the workforce, which is lower than rates for other female groups. More specifically, 71 percent of married non-Hispanic White mothers with children under age 18 are in the workforce, 82 percent of married Black mothers are in the workforce, and 66 percent of married Asian mothers also work. It *appears* on the surface that married Hispanic mothers have the lowest labor force participation of all ethnic women. I would argue that Hispanic women are not stay-at-home mothers in the traditional mainstream American sense. Instead, these Latinas, who are very industrious, and very motivated to provide the best care for their families, and who may need additional income for household living, education, and other financial goals, often complement traditional work with a second income stream. This second income stream is often found in direct selling.

The direct-selling industry that sells to consumers through independent distributors, party plans, and through network marketing, provides an effective means of generating income while balancing the needs of home and other responsibilities. Many Latinas have discovered the benefits of direct selling and many direct sellers have discovered that Latina women as excellent prospects, as well. Companies such as Avon Products, Inc., JAFRA Cosmetics, Tupperware, Princess House, and others have been successful in growing sales by recruiting and selling to Latinas.

Latinas, especially those foreign-born who may come to this country at an older age and lack the educational credentials of their U.S.-born Latina sisters, are looking for ways to create income to *supplement* their full time jobs or income to represent their *primary* means of livelihood. They, along with U.S.-born Latinas, appreciate direct selling for the greater control that it offers in work-life balance. While many corporations are making significant advancements in providing flexible work arrangements for their employees, corporations in the direct-selling industry have long recognized the value they offer independent distributors in giving them control over their work schedules.

This unique characteristic of direct selling is paying off for them with the ethnic markets, and with Latinas in particular. Today, according to the Direct Selling Association (DSA) over 15 percent of their company members' distributors are Hispanic and this number continues to grow.

LATINA LEADING VOICES INTERVIEW

On Mentoring Other Women

When I mentor younger women, I work to help them understand to be self empowered, take initiative, be smart about what you're doing, ask questions but only after you've really tried to answer them on your own. And be creative; don't let boundaries stop you; never let someone else tell you what your potential is or your capability. You know that in your heart and reach for the stars every time. And so for other women, Latina like myself, it's imperative for them to understand this as well.

For those Latinas who opt to achieve success and accomplishment in the corporate sector, there are other challenges that often characterize their journey. Josy Laza Gallagher, Senior Consultant at FutureWork Institute and First Vice President of Madrinas, an organization of Latina executives dedicated to the advancement of other Latinas in corporations comments: "Latinas have the unique challenge of language, culture, assimilation, family work/life balance, and extended family to contend with. Yet, we are essential to the foundation and growth of the corporate workplace. Success depends on a mutual exchange between corporations and Latinas to win."

Among some there is a misconception that Latinas are willing to wait until they are past a certain age to excel or that they simply don't want to advance. One Latina executive interviewed for this book stated, "Sometimes, our firms fail to see our potential, or put us in a position but never come back to see if we are interested in doing something else or something more." Another executive said that some Latinas hold themselves back from moving forward. "We are so grateful for the promotion that we don't even think to consider that there is further upward mobility." She goes on to say that mentoring becomes difficult because there are few Latinas in senior level positions in the company. As such, some Latinas seek camaraderie and support from Black women in management. Some believe that a Black woman would share the same passions for progression and advancement as a Latina and have some successful solutions to share to help climb the corporate ladder.

Building trust among women of color in the workplace is exactly what Stephanie Counts and Dee Dixon, co-founders of The Women's Intercultural Exchange (WIE) believe is necessary for success in the workplace. "We saw a strong need to examine trust among women of color. Women of color were starting businesses at a faster rate than the rest of economy; they have one trillion dollars in buying power, but they are not sitting at the corporate table. We commissioned a study of women and found that women of color had a startling level of only 22 percent trust for Caucasian women." The WIE is focused on creating partnerships in the community that build awareness and bridges of trust among Latina, Black, Asian, Native American, Caucasian and other diverse women's groups.

THINK ABOUT IT

U.S. Hispanic Women will account for a significant portion of the new workforce talent pool. How does this affect your decisions about:

Your Work Life Flexibility Programs

Do you offer work life flexibility programs for your employees? What are the participation rates by women of color ethnic groups? Latina women?

Your Employee Affinity Groups

How do you support employee affinity groups among women and diverse audiences? Is there a specific group or sub-group that addresses the needs of Latina women? How can you encourage more dialog on the issues of importance to Latina women in the workplace? Which companies should you benchmark progress against?

Recruiting & Rewarding

Are you consciously working to increase penetration of Latina talent in your workforce, within independent distributor and wholesale groups, in your supplier base? Do you have the correct compensation and reward structure in place to motivate your team to achieve business targets among diverse consumers? Do you have market awareness and training tools available (through company intranet sites, downloadable diversity tool kits, local market action planning materials) for your teams?

Dismantling myths

1. Latinas are not monolithic

Not only are Hispanics different from the point of view of country of origin, but also they differ in levels of acculturation. Highly respected research firms, such as Synovate, have done a great deal of work on the subject of acculturation. Rather than attempting to summarize this wealth of information here, I would summarize by stating that there are three distinct groups of Latinas that vary on degree of cultural adaptation, language preference, and education/affluence. It is important for companies to understand which segment has the greatest potential for its products and services.

Acculturated Hispanic women are primarily second and third generation Latinos, whose surnames are Spanish in origin. Their knowledge of Spanish may be limited, and their media preference is heavily weighted towards English-language content and programming. Approximately 55 percent of their media usage is in English (TV, radio, print). They tend to be younger, better educated, and more affluent than other groups. They represent a high degree of value to companies whose products or services are technological in nature and are higher priced.

Partially acculturated Hispanic women consume media in both English and Spanish, and are comfortable in each, spending approximately 40 percent of their time with English-language media. Importantly, both acculturated and partially acculturated Hispanics maintain strong Latino pride and retain elements of their heritage in the form of traditionally prepared foods, ethnic music, and conversational Spanish.

Unacculturated Hispanic women tend to be older and Spanish-language dominant. They are generally recent immigrants and include both older and younger women. The common unifier for unacculturated Hispanics is the lack of English-language proficiency and strong reliance on Spanish language as the basis of communication. Not surprisingly, more than 80 percent of their media is consumed in Spanish.

2. Latinas are not all Caucasian

Contrary to popular belief, Hispanics are not all Caucasian and fair skinned with straight hair. There are U.S. Latinos and Latinas who are light-skinned, brown-skinned, dark-skinned, have kinky, wavy, and straight hair, and both broad and narrow facial features. Similarly, there are Hispanics with blonde hair, blue eyes, and fair, Caucasian skin. There is a world of Afro Latinos that lies *beyond the stereotypes* that are portrayed in the media and in advertising. And I, along with 11 million other U.S. Latinas, am in that mixed in-between world of African-descended Hispanics. This does not include an additional 10 to 11 million Latino men in the U.S. who claim mixed African ancestry.

According to the U.S. Census Bureau, 44.5 percent of all Hispanics indicated they were of "mixed" racial heritage, and an additional 2 percent claimed African ancestry. From a historical perspective, only 5 percent of the African slaves that were traded during the Middle passage were sent to the United States; 95 percent were sent to South America, Mexico and the Caribbean. The first slaves to arrive in the Western Hemisphere went to Hispañola—today's Dominican Republic —not Virginia. And, they arrived 100 years *earlier* than they did in the United States. So the impact and influence of African people, customs, music, and food is *infused* in Latino culture. Dr. Marta Vega, President and Founder of the Caribbean Cultural Center in New York has done extensive research on the African Diaspora experience. I encourage you to contact her organization (*www.cccadi.org*) for more information. Also, *www.vidaafrolatina.com* and *www.caoba.org* are two websites that provide lifestyle and product information for Afro Latinos—in both English and Spanish.

From a marketing point of view, this audience of Afro Latinos has unique product needs and preferences that are more closely aligned with the African-American market (cosmetics, skin care, hair care, toiletries, shaving products, music, fashion), yet the culture and language is in tune with the Hispanic market. They are a segment that straddles more than one audience and cannot be pigeonholed into one group. Companies who are proactive and looking for untapped and under-served markets need look no further.

- Globally there are over 150 million male and female persons of Afro-Latino descent. Approximately 22 million live in the U.S.

- U.S. Afro Latinas will grow approximately 13 percent by 2010 to almost 12.7 million. For perspective, this is as large as the current Asian-American population.

- The economic buying power of U.S. Afro Latinas was estimated at $160 billion in 2005.

- U.S. Afro Latinas will control an estimated $215 billion in economic buying power by 2012—a 34 percent increase over 2005 levels.

- If U.S. Afro Latinas were a country, their economic buying power in 2012 would rank them #31 on the World Economic GDP Rank, ahead of countries like: Argentina ($214 billion), Portugal ($193 billion), and Venezuela ($182 billion).

LATINA LEADING VOICES INTERVIEW

On Latina Stereotypes

There's a stereotype of Latina women as great housekeepers, possibly that being their occupation; stay-at-home moms. That may be true for some but it's not true for all. These are intelligent, career-minded women; very entrepreneurial. They'll go out, open a business, be very diligent in pursuing a business and be very independent.

The amount of money that companies leave on the table because they do not understand Latinas is unimaginable because Latinas are aspirational; they have big dreams and they'll try very hard to attain those dreams. They've worked for so long in the home and with the family and placed so many things in priority that now they're looking at putting themselves on the path to achievement. And they're doing it; they're doing it in big numbers and they need to be reckoned with because they're an audience that comprises a large portion of your marketplace . . . So, I think that's the reality versus the stereotype America has of us Latina women.

---

3. *Latinas can be reached using English language and digital, non-traditional media.*

While Spanish-dominant Latinas are an important group to market and sell to, there is a growing acknowledgement among media and marketing companies of the English-dominant and bi-lingual Latina, and the need to create targeted strategies and programs to reach her. According to the National Survey of Latinos, 25 percent of all Hispanics are English-dominant, 28 percent are bi-lingual, and 47 percent are Spanish-dominant. Therefore, marketers have the opportunity to reach Latinas in general market media using relevant advertising strategies and content that has cultural relevance. Lifestyle situations, talent, music, and themes that appeal to bi-lingual and English dominant Latinas will be most effective. The Internet offers great value in reaching Latinas, especially U.S.-born Latinas. Studies show that acculturation, language, and education play a role in Hispanic Internet use, with a higher degree of involvement among U.S. born Hispanics and lower involvement among Spanish-dominant Hispanics, although this segment is growing. According to a study released by Pew Hispanic Center:

- Seventy-eight percent of Latinos who are English-dominant and 76 percent of bilingual Latinos use the Internet, compared with 32 percent of Spanish-dominant Hispanic adults.

- Seventy-six percent of U.S.-born Latinos go online, compared with 43 percent of those born outside the U.S.

- Eighty-nine percent of Latinos who have a college degree, 70 percent of Latinos who completed high school, and 31 percent of Hispanic adults who did not complete high school go online.

- Mexicans, the largest national origin group in the U.S. Latino population, are among the least likely to go online: 52 percent of Latinos of Mexican descent use the Internet.

- One in four Hispanics has visited YouTube, which is comparable to the general markets. But among Latinas, according to Synovate Research, only 20 percent had visited the site, compared with 41 percent of Latino men.

- Some Latinos who do not use the Internet are connecting to the communications revolution via cell phone. Fully 59 percent of Latino adults have a cell phone and 49 percent of Latino cell phone users send and receive text messages on their phones.

Best practices in reaching Latinas

Chapter nine provides a detailed action plan on how to access the growth potential of the women-of-color markets. Suffice to say that having top level CEO commitment and visible engagement to diversity remains the number one "best practice" in generating incremental market share among diverse consumers. This commitment must clearly come from the top, be reinforced in regular business planning and sales tracking meetings, and be validated through budgets, which are aligned with the diversity business case. Chapter nine will begin with this basic foundational tenet and provide more in-depth advice on how to deepen your relationship with the U.S. Latina market. Also, you will find checklists and reference tools in the Appendix of this book, which will be helpful as you craft an action plan to grow your business among this target.

We've covered a great deal in this chapter and armed you with vital information about the strength of the Hispanic women's market as a true gold mine of opportunity for companies across many different industries. Let's now turn our attention to the African American woman—a consumer audience that generates more economic buying power than Latina and Asian women combined!

FIVE

Black Voices of the African Diaspora

STRONG. PROUD. INDEPENDENT. These are some of the words used to describe the 21 *million* females of African descent who live in the United States. They have overcome centuries of institutional roadblocks, have broken through years of alienation in corporate America, in politics, and in the field of education, and yet often remain marginalized as consumers. As one research participant stated, "Black women are on the margins of the margins."

Yet, the African-American woman is one of the *most* critical, *fastest* growing, most *influential* segments in the consumer marketplace. She is the stalwart of the community, the pillar of the Black Church, and the anchor of every Black family. She has prayed children through many dark situations, used her faith to remain steadfast in the promise of more, and contrary to some beliefs, stands behind her Black man. She is finding her place in America's corporate boardrooms and in the 547,000 businesses she owns and manages. If there is a need for coalition building around issues that are salient to the advancement of African-American people, Black women will forge ahead, take action, and get the job done.

The tenacity and success of Black women is heralded in the arts, education, government, sports, business, and in other competitive fields. Women such as Oprah Winfrey have opened doors that transcend race in media and entertainment; women such as Susan Rice, senior political advisor for President Barack Obama, Rhodes Scholar, and Ambassador to the United Nations amaze us with their brilliance and passion. Women such as Venus and Serena Williams show us the power of determination and strategy. Along with these highly accomplished women, we have witnessed one of the highest levels of Black female ascension with the first

African-American First Lady in the White House: Michelle Obama.

This chapter is intended to put into perspective the critical facts about Black women, to dismantle myths, and to showcase their power as vital members of *The 85% Niche*. In more ways than one, African-American women are the *jewel in the crown* of women of color.

BLACK LEADING VOICES INTERVIEW

Generational Gains Among African-Descended Women

The buying power of the African American community has increased tremendously, especially when you think of more African Americans going to college, going into higher education and business ownership. Even when I begin to think just about my own personal life, I'm the *fourth generation out of slavery*. And when I think of just that and put it into context in terms of just how my own family has accumulated assets over the years—whether it's homeownership, whether we have started our businesses—there is increase in the buying power in the African-American community.

Black women "Leading Voices" snapshot

With more than 38 million persons, African Americans were the dominant "minority" market in America until a few years ago. The rapidly growing Hispanic population displaced them to second position. Many marketers almost immediately shifted strategic focus to the Hispanic market, reducing budgets and re-allocating program and people resources from the African-American market to the exploding Hispanic market.

In the process of doing so, marketers failed to recognize the dynamics that were operating below the radar with the African-American market. They failed to recognize that Black women, a 21 million-population audience, were growing 40 percent faster than the entire women's market (Figure 5.1). They also failed to understand that although the entire Hispanic market had eclipsed the African-American market in size, *Black women were virtually equal in size to the U.S. Latina market* (Figure 5.2). And, if their target audience was the group aged 18 and older—the segment responsible for brand selection, purchase decisions, and word-of-mouth referrals—they completely missed the fact that Black women remained the majority consumer market over Latinas *and other women of color in this critical age segment*—by more than half a million persons.

Here's the data to support these findings. There are approximately 700,000 more Latina females in this country than there are Black females. However, because the Hispanic population skews younger, there are 1.3 million more Latinas than Black females in the segment under age 18. Conversely, there are 570,000 *more* African-American women over age 18 in this country relative to Latina women. (Figure 5.3) This is the audience that is actively shopping, buying products, making referrals for your business, driving revenues for your company, and seeking career opportunities. Therefore, depending on your target audience, you may have a business opportunity equally as large, if not larger, in the African-American market as you do in the Latina market. Companies that reduced or displaced resources from African-American women without a full examination of the demographic trends made a serious mistake in strategy. However, it's not too late to re-balance strategies to ensure you reach both audiences with maximum power and impact. Just incorporate some of the principles in this book to leverage your business further.

Black women, 18+ are the majority consumer market, larger than Latinas and other women of color groups

▶ Figure 5.1   Population and growth trends

	2007	2000	% Growth
Latina	21,980,731	17,144,023	28.2%
Black	**21,286,017**	**19,461,176**	**9.4**
Asian American	8,291,405	6,623,231	25.2
Asian	*7,784,432*	*6,172,636*	*26.1*
Native Hawaiian/Pacific Islander	*506,973*	*450,595*	*12.5*
American Indian/Native Alaskan	2,292,162	2,136,916	7.3
Total women of color *(Includes all females of color in U.S.)*	53,850,315	45,365,346	18.7
Total U.S. Females	152,962,259	143,368,343	6.7

Source: U.S. Census Bureau

▶ **Figure 5.2   Segments, females of color**

	% Total women of color
Latina	40.8%
Black	39.5
Asian American	15.4
Asian	*14.5*
Native Hawaiian/Pacific Islander	*0.9*
American Indian/Native Alaskan	4.3
Total women of color	100
(Includes all females of color in U.S.)	

Source: U.S. Census Bureau

▶ **Figure 5.3   Segments by age, 2007**

	Hispanic	Black	
Female	**21,980,731**	**21,286,017**	
Under 18 years	**7,532,461**	**6,187,684**	*+1.3MM Hispanic females under the age of 18 vs. Black females*
Under 5 years	2,404,500	1,755,104	
5 to 13 years	3,616,222	2,977,211	
14 to 17 years	1,511,739	1,455,369	
18 to 64 years	**13,008,784**	**13,076,121**	
18 to 24 years	2,398,783	2,299,498	*570, 000 more Black women 18+ versus Latina women*
25 to 44 years	6,876,981	6,026,260	
45 to 64 years	3,733,020	4,750,363	
65 years and over	**1,439,486**	**2,022,212**	

Source: U.S. Census Bureau

BLACK LEADING VOICES INTERVIEW

On Black Female Stereotypes

Even though we are a powerful buying unit, there are still myths about the African-American woman and the African-American family. One that comes to mind is in terms of buying new cars. As I walked into a car dealership, it's amazing that I walked out of one equally as fast when they asked whether my husband was going to co-sign. They made an assumption about me . . . about my buying power. And certainly that's a myth that we have to begin to dispel.

Age

Like Latina women, Black women are younger than their general market counterparts as evidenced in the age cohort analysis below. Data from the U.S. Census shows that Black women are younger than women by 10 years, with a median age of 32 years (versus 42 years). The youthfulness of the African-American women's market represents competitive advantage to companies that seek new first-time users and to those whose products skew young. The hair care market is an excellent example of an industry that is largely dependent upon the purchase selection process of young Black women. The heavy use of hair care (maintenance products, chemical relaxers, color, and styling aids), a tendency to remain loyal to products that deliver the desired results on Black hair, and frequent changes in contemporary hair styling all contribute to sales.

The segment aged 25 to 44 is a particularly strong "sweet spot" for the African-American woman's market. Nearly 29 percent of all Black females cluster in this segment compared with about to 25 percent of women overall. This is an excellent target for companies seeking to expand their employee base and reach well-educated emerging talent.

The segment aged 25 to 44 is also the group that makes large, high ticket purchase decisions—such as buying a first automobile or a home. Within the automotive industry, for example, 58 percent of all new vehicle purchases made by African Americans are made by women. This is well over the 45 percent new vehicle purchase level reported among women in general. And, at approximately $30,000 per new car, truck, or crossover vehicle purchased, this incremental purchase rate pays off in huge revenue streams, not to mention the on-going service business associated with new vehicle purchases.

At the other extreme of the age spectrum, there are fewer Black women approaching retirement age than in the general market women's segment. Only 9.6 percent of Black women are aged 65 and over, compared with 17.4 percent of women in general. These 2 million Black women who are nearing retirement are taking a different view towards life. Research by Ariel Capital Management shows that African Americans approaching retirement years are *three times more likely* than their Caucasian counterparts to consider starting a new business as they approach retirement. Companies have a huge opportunity to coach these women in their pre-retirement years with low risk, high reward entrepreneurial choices to satisfy their dreams. Businesses that require little up front capital investment, yet can produce a good income stream will be particularly appealing to pre-retirement women of African descent.

▶ Figure 5.4   Black women by age segment, 2007

	Black	Women of color	Non-Hispanic White
Female	21,286,017	53,850,315	101,346,238
Under 18 years	**29.0%**	**30.4%**	**20.2%**
Under 5 years	8.2	9.1	5.4
5 to 13 years	14..0	14.6	9.9
14 to 17 years	6.8	6.7	4.9
18 to 64 years	**61.4%**	**61.4%**	**62.4%**
18 to 24 years	10.8	10.7	8.7
25 to 44 years	28.3	30.4	25.4
45 to 64 years	22.3	20.3	28.3
65 years and over	**9.6%**	**8.2%**	**17.4%**
Median age (years)	32.0	31.2	42.1

Source: U.S. Census Bureau

Education

Black women are making steady gains in closing the learning gap and enjoying the access provided by higher education. Over the past 33 years, Black women have enrolled in four-year colleges at higher rates than have Black men, according to the results of a study conducted by the Higher Education Research Institute at UCLA's Graduate School of Education and Information Studies. In 2004, Black women comprised 59 percent of all first-time, full-time Black students attending four-year institutions, compared with 54.5 percent in 1971.

Educational aspirations remain high. Twenty-four percent of Black students intend to obtain doctoral degrees, as compared with 17 percent of the general population of students. Black students also were slightly more likely to express interest in professional degrees than were students overall—medical degrees (12 percent vs. 9 percent) and law degrees (6 percent vs. 5 percent). Black women were twice as likely (16 percent) to aspire toward medical degrees than were men (8 percent). This gender difference is more pronounced among Black students than in the general student population interested in medical careers (11 percent of women vs. 7 percent of men). Overall, Black women more than doubled the number receiving a Master's Degree over the 10-year time period from 1991 to 2001, as shown in Figure 5.5.

▶ **Figure 5.5   Master's Degrees**

	1991	2001	% Change
African-American women	10,700	26,697	+149.5%
White women	146,813	194,487	+32.5
White men	114,419	125,993	+10.1

Source: National Center for Education Statistics, U.S. Department of Education, Digest of Educational Statistics, 2002

While the educational attainment of Black women is to be applauded, this fact led two executives I interviewed to share their views on the implications for the future.

Bea Y. Perdue, Executive Director, The Johnetta B. Cole Global Diversity and Inclusion Institute at Bennett College suggests Black women's access to higher education is fueled, in part, by a view that they are less threatening than Black men with degrees:

"Education among Black women is on a huge rise. On the one hand, we say 'It's about time', but on the other hand, you ask about your men. When you look at kids and how they are being socialized and how they are being taught and not being taught, you have to theorize that women are less threatening than men. [Black] women are going to get the access and opportunity because they are viewed as less threatening than Black men."

And, Linda Forte, Senior Vice President of Business Affairs for Comerica Bank, discussed the available marriage pool, the educational attainment of Black women, and their implications for future relationships between Black men and women:

"If those trends [educational attainment] continue the implications are that many of our women will think about age, whom they interact with, and who they marry. We will see women seeking opportunities to become involved in relationships that are inside the race. I have a sense that we will see Black women be open to multicultural relationships ... we will also see Black women who marry those without same educational attainment. Their options are to stay within their race or marry "down" from an economic point of view."

The observations of Ms. Perdue and Ms. Forte are both valid and important, and warrant further examination and monitoring from a broader sociological and psychographic perspective.

Economic picture: money and affluence

Money

Black women's influence in the marketplace has grown since the early 1980s. With over $524 billion in buying power in 2007, they are clearly in control of the pocketbook and the decisions of the family. By 2010 based on $1.1 trillion in buying power for all African Americans, this number will swell to over $682 billion. They represent 55 percent of all African Americans in this country, but according to a recent *MSNBC Nightly News* "Report on the State of Black Women in America," they generate 62 percent of all African-American wealth. No other woman-of-color segment commands this prestigious economic position. The buying power of Black women is larger than the buying power of Latina and Asian women—combined. On a per capita basis, Black women are responsible for generating $24,952 annually versus $12,909 among Latinas and $16,625 among Asian-American women.

▶ **Figure 5.6   Women-of-color buying power, per capita, 2007**

	Economic buying power	Population	$ per capita
Black	$524 billion	21 million	$24,952
Latina	$284 billion	22 million	$12,909
Asian	$133 billion	8 million	$16,625

Source: U.S. Census Bureau, Selig Center, *Packaged Facts*

BLACK LEADING VOICES INTERVIEW

On Product Purchase Decisions

If I find a product that really speaks to my needs, I tend to stick with that product. And if there's a shift in terms of whether they have not made improvements in that particular product, I share that with the company as well. Because I feel that they need to continuously improve the product. If I have a good thing, I continue to stay with it and I share it with my friends because I want them to know how I feel about that product—whether it's purchasing a car or whether it is an article of clothing. I think it's very significant that we as African American women support products that work well for us and that we give feedback to the company; they should continue to value us as consumers as well. When I find a company that addresses my needs I share that with my friends.

If a company does *not* meet my expectations as an African-American woman in my community I sever the ties with that company and my style is, I don't go back. I look for someone or another company that could provide my needs and services within my community. You *don't get a second chance;* you've already demonstrated to me that you don't want my business, that you don't want my dollars. That's why I really believe that if you're doing a good job, if you're being a good corporate citizen, I want to tell that story. I want to help you be successful. If you're not being a good corporate steward, then you need to move on because you don't get a second chance, especially when you're working with a grassroots community, because there's an *erosion of trust* there that cannot be restored.

Yet, somehow despite these figures, the recognition of African-American women as a pivotal, deciding consumer audience with almost twice as much spending power as any other woman-of-color group has not been met with the open arms of businesses. Companies are either unaware of the facts surrounding the power of Black women or are in denial about the significant influence that Black women have on their businesses. Some may take Black women for granted, believe that they are automatically reaching them in their multicultural marketing or marketing-to-women strategies, or believe they can rest on their loyalty for years to come without making any changes to business strategies. This could not be further from the truth. Others may have an old, misguided perception of Black women, shaped by years of typecasting. As one research participant who requested to remain anonymous noted: ". . . Stop watching the 10 o'clock news and BET . . . if you were to only see [these television programs] you would not see the full scope of African-American women."

BLACK LEADING VOICES INTERVIEW

On Opportunities in the Financial Products Industry

The biggest thing for us is how, in the African-American community, that we, especially women can still continue to increase our financial literacy. More and more, we're outliving our husbands. I tend to think that maybe I didn't get started in the game early enough, but there's still time for me to prepare towards my retirement. I continue to go to workshops and to bring my friends to bounce ideas off of them and become more creative with finances.

Affluence

We've already noted that Black women represent more disposable income than any other women-of-color segment. Further, we've demonstrated that on a per-capita basis, Black women outnumber women of color nearly 2:1 in economic clout. Let's turn our attention now to affluence and the upscale women-of-color market.

There are certain geographic markets where upscale Black families—those earning $200,000 plus—are more likely to live. These markets are New York, Washington, D.C., Chicago, Los Angeles, Atlanta, Detroit, Philadelphia, San Francisco, Dallas, and Baltimore. Together, these ten metro markets account for 51 percent of all African-American households with a woman present and with incomes in excess of $200,000 per year. The combined total annual gross income of these markets is well over 10 billion dollars. If your products are upscale in nature or if you seek to drive brand consideration among an influential segment of the Black female population these are the geographic strongholds where you will want to concentrate resource and planning efforts.

▶ Figure 5.7   Metro areas where most affluent African Americans are found

number of Black households with incomes above $200,000

New York	13,042
Washington, D.C.	6,040
Chicago	5,923
Los Angeles	4,657
Atlanta	4,171
Detroit	4,141
Philadelphia	3,148
San Francisco	2,353
Dallas	2,271
Baltimore	2,122
Total	43,727

Source: U.S. Census Bureau, 2004

Here are some other important statistics about the affluence of Black women and their households:

- While the African-American household income is lower than the U.S. average, the percentage of black households with incomes of $50,000 or more grew 13 percent between 2003 and 2007, compared with 8.4 percent for total U.S. households.

- There are 2.4 million affluent African-American households with incomes of $75,000 or more. They account for 17 percent of all African-American households, but 45 percent of total African American buying power.

- The 2006 annual median earnings of African Americans, over age 15 who worked full time—men: $34,770, women: $30,352.

Purchasing power

The purchasing power of Black women spans many categories and industries:

- 7.6 million African Americans said they exercise regularly at home, which opens up markets for fitness items.
- 3.9 million Black women spend $150 per week on groceries.
- African-American men and women represent 22 percent and 26 percent, respectively, of all suit buyers, casual clothes, and other apparel.
- Companies offering luxury items and financial services are positioned to market to affluent African Americans who are disproportionate buyers of luxury items such as cruise ship vacations, new cars, designer clothes, and life insurance.
- A high proportion of African Americans shop at convenience-oriented formats, such as dollar, drug, and convenience/gas stores.
- Nearly half (46 percent) of African-American households shop at beauty supply stores, almost three times the rate for non-African-American households.
- Cosmetics, hair care products and personal care products along with clothes, continue to be the top items purchased among Black women in the United States.

▶ Figure 5.8   Aggregate median spending of African-American households by category, 2005 and 2010 projected

Category	2005 (in millions)	2010 Projected (in millions)
Food at home	$33,600	$36,000
Food away from home	$17,000	$18,200
Alcoholic beverages	$2,200	$2,300
Housing	$133,600	$143,100
Apparel & Services	$20,300	$21,700
Transportation	$63,900	$68,500
Health care	$16,600	$17,800
Entertainment	$12,700	$13,600
Personal care	$5,800	$6,200
Reading	$700	$800
Education	$5,400	$5,800

Category	2005 (in millions)	2010 Projected (in millions)
Tobacco products	$2,200	$2,300
Cash contributions	$10,500	$11,200
Personal insurance	$31,500	$33,700
Miscellaneous	$5,800	$6,200
All Combined	$361,800	$387,400

Sources: Based on Selig Center Median HH Expenditures and U.S. Census HH Projections

Geography

Geographically, the African-American female population is concentrated in the top ten markets of New York (10 percent), Chicago (5 percent), Los Angeles (4 percent), Atlanta (4 percent), Washington, D.C. (4 percent), Philadelphia (4 percent), Detroit (3 percent), Houston (3 percent), Miami (2 percent), and Dallas (2 percent). Focused marketing and sales plans in these markets, working with local sales teams will result in higher levels of success.

THINK ABOUT IT

African-American women are a $500+ billion consumer market. How does this affect your decisions about:

Your Multicultural Marketing Plan
What changes to your multicultural ethnic plan, if you have one in place, are necessary to ensure you are connecting with Black women? What assumptions have you made about this market segment that have cost you several points of lost market share? What adjustments to your women's marketing plan will you make as a result of this knowledge?

Your Product Portfolio
Does your current product line include features and benefits that address the unique physiological and aspirational needs of Black women? How robust is your new product development process in addressing the needs of diverse women of color? Do you factor these market segments into your planning process at the early stages of development, or do you qualify results with other customer groups after product plans are in place?

continues . . .

> **Your Sales Expectations**
>
> Do you have a specific sales target in mind when focusing on African American customers? Do you have the internal infrastructure and data-base models to retrieve gender and ethnicity sales? If so, how well are you performing to expectation? What changes are needed to stay ahead of the growth curve of the Black women's market?
>
> **Your Workforce**
>
> Are you working to create a workforce that mirrors the African-American female market? What plans do you have in place to recruit more Black women into your workforce?

African-American marriage and family

Family is a cornerstone of the African-American community. Even though only 31 percent of Black women are married versus 44 percent of women of color and 52 percent of all women, the integrity of the family unit and how children are raised are important differentiators in the African-American community. The fact that there are more Black women who have never been married than those who have been with a partner has its root in the history of the slave trade and in the systematic efforts to dismantle the Black family structure. Husbands, wives, and children were sold indiscriminately, leading to a greater need for self-reliance and independence among African Americans. Mothers were left to raise those left behind and the family unit was dissolved.

African Americans have sought to transcend this history through strong family values. For example, children take on a greater respon-sibility for household chores since moms are invariably working full time, some are in school, and as reported earlier, many Black mothers are single-head-of-household parents. The Black woman is time pressed and consumed with responsibility in a way that most women cannot begin to comprehend. In spite of the heavy load she carries, she wants to ensure that she provides balance, discipline and opportunity to her children and does so in a way that will set a strong foundation for future success.

There is a segment of the Black population that has been successful in achieving this goal. Listen to this excerpt from and interview with

Ms. Bea Y. Perdue, Executive Director, The Johnetta B. Cole Global Diversity and Inclusion Institute at Bennett College, as she sheds light on this point of raising Black children:

Miriam Muléy: "Can you share a bit with me on your thoughts of Black parenting styles?"

Bea Perdue: "When I talk to young women they say, "My mom is my best friend." Yet it is that intersection [of age, relationship and responsibility] that is inappropriate. For me my mother became my friend when I was much older. At 14 she was a parent . . . not a friend. They [parent and child] are too different to be one and the same. A lot of our young girls are not getting that [distinction]. Parents need to be parents.

"We were much more disciplinarian [as Black parents] in practice. You ask, 'what's going to become of these young women?' You say to these people, 'you need to be more team oriented, you have so much promise but every time someone brings your weaknesses to your attention, you get a reputation for being unapproachable, you get passed over for promotions.' You see the root from where it comes from . . . the lack of discipline."

Muléy: "Our generation is not being given the tough love that our parents gave to us growing up. Would you agree or disagree with that?"

Perdue: "Every family wants their children to do better than their generation. They wanted us to have access and opportunity. Education and access are the great equalizers. They didn't want us to have to fight as hard as they did. We want the same thing for our children. But *we lose some of the lesson* . . . the lesson of being on time and staying on task. It is not so much about getting up at 5 a.m. to start chores or walk to school as some of us or our parents may have had to do, but there is a lesson there. What were our parents really teaching? So when you get to a job and you are always late people translate that to *lack of commitment.* 'She's always the last one here.' We must translate the core values our parents taught us into the new things . . . that's where we're losing."

BLACK LEADING VOICES INTERVIEW

On Challenges in the Retail Process and Community Building

As a consumer, what I'd like for you to know about me as an African-American consumer, is that I make my own decisions; that I still feel very strongly that you have to make it attractive to me and to really come and to think about me as a consumer in my community as well. Don't hesitate to outreach the African-American woman or the African Americans in our community. Come in to our community, get to know us, get to know our needs because there's no question about it, that we have the income more and more and we're continuing to gather assets. If you want to reach us, make us feel that our dollars and our voice is heard and counted.

From my perspective we are looking for a long-term relationship; we're looking at community building . . . a long-term commitment versus short term. We're not looking for a carpetbagger to come in to take from our community, we're looking for someone, a corporation to come in and make that long-term investment and be willing to work with us.

Before I open up that checking account to some of the financial institutions in that community, I want to know what they have invested in that community. What's their rate on mortgages in the community? Many companies or financial institutions are seeing a need to come more into the African-American community but our expectations are not only that you come in and build that building, but also that we know what kind of citizen are you going to be as a part of that community. We're also expecting jobs. We're also expecting not just entry jobs but we expect management positions—whether it's car insurance to mortgages. Help us; take a risk. You won't be disappointed.

▶ **Figure 5.9   African-American marital status**

	Black	Women of color	All women 15+
Married	31.2%	44.2%	52.2%
Divorced	12.8	10.1	10.8
Widowed	10.4	7.8	10.5
Separated	5.9	4.6	2.5
Never Married	39.7	33.5	24.0
Total Single	68.8	55.8	47.8

Source: U.S. Census Bureau

Another important aspect of the Black family life experience that enables Black women to raise families and defy the odds is their ability to endure great burdens and to do so with grace and courage. "Grace under fire" well defines the Black female experience. One expression of this trait is found in our ability to take on responsibility without visibly flinching. As an example, African-American women (and women of color) created the concept of "multi-tasking" long before Caucasian women understood its need or meaning. There was no such thing as "work life balance" in earlier times, or taking time off to be on the "mommy track" without the risk that one's career would be compromised in the process. These are luxuries White women would later fight for as they entered the work force in the early 1970s.

African-American women have *always* worked and *always* raised a family; the majority still does so today. They sometimes cared for two families if you consider the days when many Black women were housekeeper and nanny to other children, or when Black grandmothers were taking care of grandchildren, nieces, and nephews while managing to tend to their homes, serve as volunteers at church services, visit ailing family members, and even work a steady job.

Multitasking in the Black community was simply about having a vision for the future and being steadfast to that vision—whether that vision was sending their children to college or buying a home. It was about working smarter, and delegating responsibility. Often that delegation was directed to the children—the oldest child would cook and make sure the younger children did their chores, were playing in an area where they could be seen and quickly called in, and did their homework after school.

I can recall growing up in New York City that all our friends' parents worked—Black or Puerto Rican. *The Donna Reed Show* was wonderful—but that's what it was: a "show." Although entertaining, it was far removed from the realities of our youth. Our mothers were not home in aprons, baking cookies, or attending PTA meetings. They were working one, or sometimes two, jobs to make ends meet and raising us at the same time. Our mothers set a powerful role model for us by establishing the expectation that one could work *and* raise a family—we could have it all, if we were organized and had a plan. And so, the thought of being a stay-at-home mother never, ever seriously entered my mind growing up.

Make no mistake. Black women have *always* been at the lead and have *always* been the pillar of the Black family, rallying children, supporting their mates, and remaining connected to the community.

Country of origin

Like the Hispanic and Asian populations, there is tremendous diversity within the African-American culture. I've discussed in some detail my Afro-Puerto Rican roots. In addition to the $400 billion U.S. Afro-Latino population, there are other immigrant groups that comprise the larger landscape of the Black American experience. According to the U.S. Census, 8 percent of all African Americans are first-generation immigrants of African ancestry; an additional 10 percent are second or third generation African ancestry. Of those born outside the U.S., 50 percent are from the Caribbean, including Jamaica, Trinidad, Tobago, Haiti, and other islands. The remaining Black immigrants are from the continent of Africa. Foreign-born African Americans are spread throughout the U.S., however major concentrations exist in California, New York, Florida, and Nevada.

A Snapshot: Jamaican Americans

Marketers who want to grow market share among an audience with financial means or have business opportunities on the East Coast should strongly consider localized brand strategies to engage Jamaican women and their families. While it is difficult to confirm the exact number of Jamaicans and women of Jamaican ancestry in this country, the U.S. Census Bureau projects the number of documented Jamaican Americans at 435,000. When adjusted for illegal immigration and numbers of individuals who choose not to respond to census inquiries, the Jamaican population is more likely estimated at 1 million persons living in the United States. Women make up roughly half of that number.

- Specific estimates of actual buying power among Jamaicans are not readily available; however, we know that many Jamaicans are working-class Americans. They own many successful businesses in the communities in which they live (grocery stores, restaurants, travel agencies, realtor brokerages, bakeries, bars, and beauty salons), many nurses and nurse aides are of Jamaican ancestry, and it is not unusual in cities like New York and Miami to find large groups of West Indian Americans teaching in schools and universities. Jamaican professional businesses include computer consulting and training in word processing, law firms, private medical practices, immigration agents, or counselors.

- Fifty-nine percent live in the Northeast (primarily New York's "Kingston 22" area of Brooklyn); 4.8 percent in the Midwest; 30.6 percent in the South (primarily Florida, in Miami's "Little Jamaica" area); and 5.6 percent in the West.

- Jamaican women are proud, regal women and often distance themselves from claims of being "African American" due to their cultural pride, heritage, and international distinction in sports and music. Jamaican women are the gatekeepers of family traditions, such as religion, the preparation of customary foods, respect for elders, supporting the advancement of the family, and in particular, stressing the importance of education and literacy.

- Jamaica has one of the highest literacy rates of all Caribbean countries. Education is highly valued among West Indians and Jamaican mothers will make time in their busy working schedules to take an active interest in their children's education, join school Parent Teacher Associations, attend school board meetings, and get involved in Scholastic Aptitude Test preparation support.

- Like Black women in general, Jamaican women will galvanize around important community issues, bond together, and voice concerns around local crime, racism, civic and political affairs. Community activism around relevant issues is an effective way to connect with women of Jamaican ancestry.

- The unique verbal communication and linguistic style is another

defining trait of recent arrivals to this country, as is the dress and
hairstyle (dreadlocks) of many Rastafarians—a religious group of
West Indies. Using these cultural cues and targeted media to
reach Jamaicans will help drive greater relevance and connectivity
for brands.

A Snapshot: Haitian Americans

Equal in size to the Jamaican American population are Haitian Americans. According to the U.S. Census, Haitians account for about 1 million
persons—300,000 of whom are legalized U.S. citizens. Approximately
half of the total Haitian population is comprised of women. The size
of the Haitian market, its concentrated geographic residence, unique
media and language, and strong traditions makes it a potential target
for several brands and industries.

- Heavy concentrations of Haitian families are found along the
  Eastern seacoast, including New York and Florida.

- Haitians speak *Patois*, a dialect of French although they share
  the island of Hispañola with the Dominican Republic, a Spanish-speaking country. There are several media outlets in the U.S.
  that target Haitians.

- As with other cultural groups, the family is at the center of Haitian tradition. Families consist of father, mother, children and
  grandparents. Children are expected to care for the older members of the family as they age, and like other ethnic populations,
  the concept of nursing homes is unthinkable. Senior citizens are
  treated with respect and honor and hold a high position of esteem
  in the family hierarchy. The male is considered the authoritarian
  and breadwinner, and from birth he is given more freedom and
  educational opportunities than females, although Haitian women
  play a role in influencing the household decisions.

- Once they acculturate to mainstream American values, Haitian
  women become more assertive and vocal, especially the younger
  women. Younger, urban Haitian women, who live in the U.S.,
  have adopted more liberal positions regarding work and family.

They work outside the home, enjoy some degree of freedom, and are less willing to play a subservient role to the male. They want a voice in the decision-making processes and often get it.

- Haitian-American parents are generally strict with their children, as is customary in Haiti. The adults of the family monitor the children. Adult rules are to be respected and obeyed without question. Children are expected to live at home until they are married. Haitian-American children seem to accept these customs and values despite the freer attitudes and lifestyles they see in their American counterparts. Haitian parents seek a better standard of living for their children and they want them to obtain a good formal education. They want their children to grow up to be obedient and responsible.

- Religion and faith are hallmarks of traditional Haitian values. Families are less willing to seek help from a physician—in some cases due to lack of health insurance. In others the decision is based on greater reliance on folk healers and Voodoo medicine to cure ailments. The mother or grandmother is usually responsible for diagnosing symptoms and keeping alive the traditions of the family in treating sickness. As second and third generation Haitians become acculturated to mainstream values, we find that more are open to seeking medical advice. Nonetheless, pharmaceutical companies that are interested in increasing market share among Caribbean communities should address cultural preferences for natural, holistic healing versus prescription medicine only. Key influencer strategies that include local community leaders as well as physicians should also be considered to reach this target.

- Haitian family members are dependent upon each other for financial support. One example can be found in the Haitian tradition of a rotating credit association as a way of saving money for a large ticket item. (Latinos have a similar tradition called *associa-dades* or *consorsios*.) Such associations are called in Creole *sangue, min,* or *assosie*. They rotate money to members of the association from a lump-sum fund into which each member has contributed.

Haitian immigrants, especially undocumented ones who have no bank accounts, use the *sangue* to buy homes and finance various business ventures.

Best practices in reaching Black women

The support of the top level CEO is the single most important "best practice" in generating incremental market share among diverse consumers. African-American women are no exception. Reinforcement from the top should come in the form of sales and strategy updates in business meetings, clear communication of the segment importance to business results, proportionate budgets to drive programming, and workforce integration at all levels. Once this foundational support is in place, marketers can begin to create a message of relevance with African American women by:

1. Ensuring relevant communications integration

Authentic consumer communication is the hallmark of good marketing. With consumers in greater control of advertising messages, it's important to integrate your message to African-American women in a way that they will feel welcomed and respected as consumers. Creative briefs should be designed with the intent of calling out Black women as a critical segment of the target market (if strategic planning has validated the business potential of this segment) and support the audience with relevant message insights. These insights will come from many sources: consumer attitudinal studies, ethnographic work, usage reports, research from secondary sources, and published work from books such as this.

The role of targeted ethnic media should be integrated into plans to effectively reach Black women. Their value in penetrating this audience in both a demographic as well as contextual manner is meaningful to brand planning. In addition, mainstream campaigns should work to embrace Black women as a target integrating them from a platform, talent, music, life style, and cultural point of view. Moreover, digital plays a key role in reaching Black women of all ages with highly targeted content and focused reach.

2. Reaching Black women through the community

The community plays a significant role among ethnic consumers, especially for women. Giving back to the community—to the neighborhood—rings true as a message of empowerment and support among Black women. In return, African-American women will seek those brands that have a presence in their everyday lives. Local sponsorships, events, and church functions are just some examples of ways that companies can establish a point of face-to-face connection with Black women.

Philanthropic giving to national advocacy groups, professional associations, educational, and faith-based organizations is an effective way to build consideration among Black women. The key is to ensure that there is a strong marketing component to your philanthropic efforts, before, during, and after a major national event so that your programs are leveraged from a 360-degree perspective. Full integration into the activities of the organization will maximize your results.

3. Mirroring the market with diversity

Companies that take the critical step of ensuring alignment of their workforce with their customer base—both current and new target users—will want to pay attention to creating a robust and diverse workforce. Those in the field, as well as those in the home office should reflect the dynamic multiplicity of the consumers being served for maximum results and true competitive advantage.

In addition to these fundamental best practices, chapter nine provides more action tips and suggestions to ensure your organization and brands are aligned with the business opportunity related to African-American women. I encourage you to study this chapter for greater tactical planning.

SIX

Asian American Leading Voices

Andrea Jung. Indra Nooyi. Cristine Poon. Connie Chung. Lisa Ling. Ann Curry. Kristi Yamaguchi. Michelle Kwan. Vera Wang. Tia Carrere. Lucy Liu. Margaret Cho . . .

THE LIST goes on and on. From CEO ranks of Fortune 100 businesses, to television news anchorwomen, to Olympic sports winners, to fashion, beauty and entertainment, the more than 8 million females in this country who claim Asian ancestry are shaping the dynamics of the women's market. Asian-American women are among the most accomplished, the most successful, and the most distinguished women of color, indeed, women, in this country. They exceed the personal wealth and educational levels of any other multicultural market, including the mainstream markets. And, although the smallest in population size of all women-of-color groups, Asian-American women have the highest productivity levels as measured by entrepreneurship gross sales receipts, advancement into management and professional ranks, and graduate and post graduate educational attainment.

With an estimated buying power of $133 billion (Selig Center) and an additional $54 billion in gross sales receipts as entrepreneurs (Center for Women's Business Research), Asian-American women should be one of the most sought after markets in North America. In fact, for comparison purposes, Asian women entrepreneurs generate as much business revenue as Latina and Black women business owners *combined*, although they represent only half of the total number of businesses owned by these women. Their productivity levels are well beyond the productivity of other ethnic women-owned businesses, including mainstream women. Yet, many companies miss the mark when it comes to engaging Asian-American women to consider their brands. Often this is due to the real and perceived complexities of the Asian marketplace. Language, customs, and traditions vary among Chinese, Filipino, Asian-Indian, Korean, Vietnamese, and Japanese origins. And, these groups—although the largest of all Asian cultures here in the U.S.—do not include the 206,000 Cambodians, 204,000 Pakistanis, 198,000 Laotians, 186,000 Hmongs, 150,000 Thai, 144,000 Taiwanese, 63,000 Indonesian, or 57,000 Bangladeshis that live in this country. Clearly, there is tremendous diversity in the Asian-American marketplace as noted below in Figure 6.1, but this should not hold marketers back from reaching out to Asian-American women prospects.

▶ Figure 6.1   Largest Asian-American ethnic groups, 2000

Ethnic group	ASIAN ALONE		Asian & at least one other race (i.e., Filipino-White)	Total population, alone or in any combination
	Single ethnicity	Two or more Asian ethnicities (i.e., Chinese-Vietnamese)		
Chinese	2,314,537	130,826	289,478	2,734,841
Filipino	1,850,314	57,811	456,690	2,364,815
Asian Indian	1,678,765	40,013	180,821	1,899,599
Korean	1,076,872	22,550	129,005	1,228,427
Vietnamese	1,122,528	47,144	54,064	1,223,736
Japanese	796,700	55,537	296,695	1,148,932
Cambodian	171,937	11,832	22,283	206,052
Pakistani	153,533	11,095	39,681	204,309
Laotian	168,707	10,396	19,100	198,203
Hmong	169,428	5,284	11,598	186,310
Thai	112,989	7,929	29,365	150,293
Taiwanese	118,048	14,096	12,651	144,795
Indonesian	39,757	4,429	18,887	63,073
Bangladeshi	41,280	5,625	10,507	57,412

Source: *www.asianleaders.org/profile.htm*

Despite these complexities, every business leader who is focused on growing market share should become familiar with the distinguishing characteristics of this economically and culturally vibrant audience. Asian-American women represent an important strategic target to grow customer sales. They also represent a very capable and talented employee resource pool.

ASIAN WOMEN LEADING VOICES INTERVIEW

On the Voice of Asian Women: Values, Aspirations and Needs

I think companies tend to think of the Asian community as professionals, very intelligent . . . they look at them as a "higher (quality)" marketing audience. And I think the truth really might be someplace in the middle, where not everybody is a Rhodes Scholar, not everyone is a technology whiz. Companies need to know that when they're marketing to Asian women they're marketing to a group that's very intuitive and they have a lot of compassion. I think (we Asian) women share a trust, a comfort, camaraderie of sorts. Talk to us like a normal human being, don't be condescending. Talk to us as you would anyone else and listen to our needs.

Asian-American women "Leading Voices" snapshot

There were 8.3 million Asian females in the U.S. in 2007. This number grew 25.2 percent over 2000 levels and is increasing at a rate three-and-one-half times faster than all women. Immigration is a key driver of this growth, as 69 percent of all Asians were born outside of the U.S., according to the U.S. census. A little over 15 percent of all women of color in this country can trace their origins to Asian ancestry.

▶ **Figure 6.2   Population and growth trends**

	2007	2000	% Growth
Latina	21,980,731	17,144,023	28.2%
Black	21,286,017	19,461,176	9.4
Asian American	**8,291,405**	**6,623,231**	**25.2**
Asian	*7,784,432*	*6,172,636*	*26.1*
Native Hawaiian/Pacific Islander	*506,973*	*450,595*	*12.5*
American Indian/Native Alaskan	2,292,162	2,136,916	7.3
Total women of color (Includes all females of color in the U.S.)	53,850,315	45,365,346	18.7
Total U.S. females	152,962,259	143,368,343	6.7

Source: U.S. Census Bureau

▶ **Figure 6.3   Population Mix**

	% Total women of color
Latina	40.8%
Black	39.5
Asian American	**15.4**
Asian	*14.5*
Native Hawaiian/Pacific Islander	*0.9*
American Indian/Native Alaskan	4.3
Total women of color *(Includes all females of color in the U.S.)*	100

Source: U.S. Census Bureau

Language preference

As many as 90 percent and as few as 40 percent of Asian-American adults speak their native language at home, as shown in figure 6.4. Not surprisingly, most Asians learn to speak their native language first and this skill is reinforced during language classes that are provided both after school and on weekends. As in the Hispanic market, the Asian mother has the role of reinforcing language skills at home and ensuring it is used, especially when addressing elders and parents.

Because Asian Americans retain a strong preference for communication in their native language, being able to reach Asian women and their families in their own language will help increase awareness and drive greater sales.

▶ **Figure 6.4   Asian preference for native language use**

percent who prefer native language

Vietnamese	93%
Chinese	83
Korean	81
Filipino	66
Asian Indian	55
Japanese	42

Source: A-Partnership

Age

The Asian-American population is relatively young, although it is the oldest of all the ethnic groups. In 2000, the census found that the median age of Asian Americans was 34.6 years (vs. 42.1 years for non-Hispanic Whites). Fewer are entering retirement (9.4 percent of Asian-American women are over age 65 vs. 17.4 percent of non-Hispanic White women), underscoring the vitality of the market. Despite this, Asian Americans represent the largest segment of older women of color and an opportunity for the financial services, retirement, insurance, and healthcare industries.

The opportunity to engage Asian Americans in products and services that focus on elder care is reinforced by data from the Population Resource Center. This nationwide survey found that Asian Pacific Islander families provided more care for their older relatives than did other groups. Forty-two percent of Asians surveyed helped care for or provided financial support for their parents, compared with 34 percent of Latino Americans, 28 percent of African Americans, and 19 percent of Caucasians. And, as the gatekeepers of family needs, Asian-American women will be most receptive to companies who support their desire to care for aging parents.

▶ Figure 6.5   Women of color by age

	Asian/PI	Women of color	Non-Hisp. White
Female	8,291,405	53,850,315	101,346,238
Under 18 years	**24.5%**	**30.4%**	**20.2%**
Under 5 years	7.2	9.1	5.4
5 to 13 years	12.1	14.6	9.9
14 to 17 years	5.2	6.7	4.9
18 to 64 years	**66.1%**	**61.4%**	**62.4%**
18 to 24 years	9.2	10.7	8.7
25 to 44 years	33.8	30.4	25.4
45 to 64 years	23.1	20.3	28.3
65 years and over	**9.4%**	**8.2%**	**17.4%**
Median age (years)	34.6	31.2	42.1

Source: U.S. Census Bureau

Education

Asians comprise the largest college graduate population in America. Across all levels of education, including undergraduate and postgraduate education, Asian Americans and Asian-American women over the age of 25 have a higher level of educational attainment. Forty-six percent of Asian-American men and 39 percent of Asian-American women have bachelor's degrees, compared with 39 percent of White men and 25 percent of White women. In addition, one in seven Asian Americans—one million people—has a Master's, Ph.D., medical, or law degree, as reported by the U.S. Census, and the American Council on Education.

The degree of attainment for Chinese Americans is 46.3 percent and 40.8 percent among Japanese Americans. It's no surprise then that Chinese Americans are disproportionately represented among the top research universities and the elite small liberal arts colleges. Vietnamese Americans have a college-degree attainment rate of 20 percent—half the rate for all Asian Americans. Without a doubt, the higher educational attainment among Asian Americans results in higher income levels than the general population. It also distinguishes Asian Americans within the workforce as a highly attractive talent pool.

ASIAN WOMEN LEADING VOICES INTERVIEW

On the Role of Family and the Acculturation Process

As an Asian woman, anything I've learned about the Asian culture has been things what I've read or by connecting with family. It was a directive that my grandparents wanted their children to be Americanized and I think part of the trade off there was not making the culture more a part of what we are about. And I think as I get older, it's something that I've embraced on my own . . . to figure out and see what it was and how much of (the culture) was really genetic, how much of it was really environment, how much was just my personality.

Economic picture: money and affluence

Money

Buying power among Asian Americans stands at $397 billion and will climb to $579 billion by 2010. This buying power puts the Asian-American GDP ahead of the entire economies of all but sixteen countries around the world. Among Asian-American women, the buying power is estimated at one-third, or $133 billion.

On a household basis, Asian Americans are among the most affluent demographic groups in our country. The median household income for Asians, currently at $52,626, is above the U.S. average of $42,409 and it has increased steadily above all demographic groups over the past 35 years.

Affluence

Asian Americans are two times more likely than mainstream households to be super affluent households—those earning $200,000 or more. More specifically, according to the *U.S. Statistical Abstract* for Income, Expenditure and Wealth, 2.3 percent of all U.S. households earn more than $200,000 while 4.1 percent of all Asian homes fit the criteria of economic affluence. Among the moderately affluent—those households earning $75,000 or more—35 percent of all Asians fall into this category versus 25 percent of all Americans.

Geographically the super affluent, $200,000+ Asian households are concentrated in New York, Los Angeles, San Francisco, San Jose, Chicago, Washington, D.C., Honolulu, Boston, Houston, and Philadelphia. Together, these ten metro markets account for 44 percent of all Asian households with a woman present and whose income is in excess of $200,000 per year. The combined total annual income of these markets is well over $14 billion. These are the geographic strongholds where you will want to concentrate resources and planning efforts to reach the upscale Asian woman and her family.

▶ Figure 6.7   Metro areas where most affluent Asians are found

number of Asian households with income above $200,000

New York	17,916
Los Angeles	14,055
San Francisco	10,437
San Jose	9,665
Chicago	4,726
Washington, D.C.	3,865
Honolulu	3,685
Boston	2,045
Houston	1,779
Philadelphia	1,517
Total	69,690

Source: U.S. Census Bureau, 2004

Purchasing Power

Asian households consume several products and services as noted in the projection of spending by the Selig Center for Economic Growth. The largest categories of purchase are in housing, as would be expected. Asians spend 36.3 percent of their annual income on housing expenditures compared with 32.4 percent of all Americans. Education also skews higher among Asian households, with 2.6 percent of annual income dedicated to schooling compared with only 1.6 percent for mainstream consumers. Personal insurance also ranks highly among Asian Americans, with 9.4 percent of Asian household income spent on personal insurance compared with slightly less (9.3 percent) among all Americans.

Asian Americans out-index all other ethnic groups in the use of technology-based products. Specifically, according to the Marketing Leadership Council, 57 percent of Asians research purchases online prior to making purchases and 61 percent make purchases online. The implication for marketers within the home mortgage, telecommunications, insurance, and education fields is to examine their business strategies—communication plans, promotional efforts, and distribution efforts—to ensure they are extending a personal invitation to Asian women to consider their brands. The higher preference for luxury items and the emphasis on high quality set this audience apart from others as premium buyers, representing yet another opportunity for marketers.

▶ **Figure 6.8   Aggregate median spending of Asian-American households by category, 2005 and 2010 projected**

aggregate median household spending in $millions for selected categories

	2005 (in millions)	2010 Projected (in millions)
Food at home	$14,000	$16,600
Food away from home	$13,000	$14,800
Alcoholic beverages	$1,400	$1,600
Housing	$71,500	$81,300
Apparel & Services	$7,700	$8,800
Transportation	$32,800	$37,300
Health care	$8,700	$9,900
Entertainment	$7,500	$8,500
Personal care	$2,400	$2,700
Reading	$400	$500
Education	$8,300	$9,400
Tobacco products	$600	$700
Cash contributions	$5,700	$6,500
Personal insurance	$21,000	$23,800
Miscellaneous	$2,000	$2,200
All combined	$197,000	$224,600

Sources: Based on Selig Center Median HH Expenditures and U.S. Census HH Projections

Geography

The Asian-American population is highly concentrated in large urban areas. Thirty-five percent of all Asian Americans live in Los Angeles (1.7 million), New York (1.4 million), San Francisco (1.3 million), and Honolulu (0.5 million). Large Asian-American communities can also be found in Chicago (0.4 million), Washington, D.C. (0.35 million), Seattle (0.3 million), and Boston (0.25 million).

Importantly, the ethnic composition of the Asian market varies by metro area as noted below. Chinese Americans have a dominant role in the major markets of New York, San Francisco, Los Angeles and Boston; however, Asian Indians are the stronghold in Chicago and Washington, D.C., while Filipinos are represented in large numbers in Seattle.

▶ Figure 6.9 Asian ethnic groups in the four largest Asian DMAs

	Los Angeles	New York	San Francisco	Honolulu
Chinese	25%	36%	37%	12%
Filipino	22	11	25	36
Vietnamese	14	2	12	2
Asian Indian	6	28	11	<1
Japanese	9	4	6	43
Korean	16	12	4	5
All others	5	7	5	<1
Total Asian population	1.7 million	1.4 million`	1.3 million	0.5 million

Source: U.S. Census, 2000

▶ Figure 6.10 Asian ethnic groups in key secondary markets

	Chicago	Washington, D.C.	Seattle	Boston
Chinese	18%	20%	19%	36%
Filipino	22	12	21	4
Vietnamese	4	13	15	1419
Asian Indian	31	22	6	22
Japanese	5	3	11	5
Korean	12	17	15	7
All others	8	13	11	15
Total Asian population	0.4 million	0.35 million	0.3 million	0.25 million

Source: U.S. Census, 2000

THINK ABOUT IT

Asian-American women are highly educated customers. How does this affect your decisions about:

Your Communications Plan

What changes to your communications message and methods of sophisticated information sharing can you integrate into your plans knowing that the Asian woman customer is more discriminating than your mainstream prospects? How can you keep her engaged and stimulated by your delivery methods?

Your Product Portfolio

Asian women and Asian culture emphasize the importance of high quality as a core value. How can you elevate this aspect of your product performance and clearly communicate the superior benefits of your brand versus the competition?

Your Sales Expectations

Do you have a specific sales target in mind when focusing on Asian American customers? Do you have the internal infrastructure and database models to retrieve gender and ethnicity sales? If so, how well are you performing to expectation? What changes are needed to stay ahead of the growth curve of the Asian women's market?

Your Workforce

Are you working to leverage the broad and deep experiences that Asian American women bring to the workforce? How can you recruit and retain more Asian women to consider joining your company? Your distributor base?

Marriage and family

Marriage is highly revered in the Asian culture and this fact is reflected in the high number of Asian-American married couples in the United States. Compared with 44.2 percent of all women of color who are married and 52 percent of all women, 60 percent of Asian women fall into this category of marital status. Conversely, fewer Asian-American women are single (never married, divorced, or widowed) compared with women of color and all women.

Psychographically, most middle-class Chinese Americans place the highest priority on raising and maintaining the family: providing for the immediate members of the family (grandparents, parents, and children), acquiring an adequate and secure home for the family, and investing time and annual income in their children's education. Among Asian Indians, men traditionally handle financial matters in the household; however women are increasingly involved in influencing decisions. The Vietnamese tend to think of the family as including maternal and paternal grandparents, uncles, aunts, and cousins. Even when adult children marry and leave the household, parents often encourage them to live nearby to maintain family ties.

ASIAN WOMEN LEADING VOICES INTERVIEW

On Male-Dominated Asian Societies

In the Asian culture it's always been very male-dominated and women always took a subservient position. And I think now what you will see is a tremendous change. It's a 180-degree change. And I think it's just being a product of living in the United States. The world is changing and everything is so different. For Asian women in particular, coming from a different culture to the United States, they find freedom that they maybe didn't have before.

▶ Figure 6.11   Asian American marital status

	Asian-American	Women of color	All women 15+
Married	60.0%	44.2%	52.2%
Divorced	5.4	10.1	10.8
Widowed	6.9	7.8	10.5
Separated	1.6	4.6	2.5
Never married	26.1	33.5	24.0
Total single	40.0	55.8	47.8

Source: U.S. Census Bureau

Country of origin

The single largest challenge companies face in reaching the Asian-American market is in recognizing that it is not monolithic. The Asian population covers a range of ethnicities, cultures, and languages. Asian Americans also vary in terms of immigration and refugee experiences, acculturation levels, and socioeconomic levels. Within the U.S. there are several Asian groups. Six of the largest are Chinese (25 percent of all Asians), Filipinos (18 percent), Asian-Indians (16 percent), Vietnamese (11 percent), Korean (10 percent), and Japanese (8 percent). Understanding the rich diversity that exists within each group and creating marketing and sales plans which cater to distinct audience needs is fundamental to success in the Asian-American market.

However, despite this diversity, there are common values among Asians that emanate from Eastern philosophies: Buddhism, Confucianism, and Taoism. They emphasize harmony, balance in relationships, respect for elders and ancestors, order, and education. Conflict is addressed, but the preference is always to do so with the utmost respect and decorum. Self control, placing other's needs ahead of one's own, deference to authority, and restraint are all hallmarks of Asian culture.

A Snapshot: Chinese Americans

Marketers who want to grow market share among the largest of all Asian groups (3.3 million) will want to concentrate on Chinese Americans. They are comprised of immigrants from four distinct areas: Taiwan, Hong Kong, PRC (Mainland China), and South East Asia, and divided into two major dialect groups: Mandarin and Cantonese.

- The major geographic concentration is in New York (504,000), San Francisco (481,000), and Los Angeles (425,000).

- Chinese Americans are highly educated and affluent with a median household income of $51,444 vs. $52,616 median Asian-American household income.

- Psychographically and according to Jane Hyun, author of *Breaking the Bamboo Ceiling*, Chinese Americans tend to be cautious in personal and business dealings. They are price conscious. They tend to plan for the long term, have respect for authority and elders, and seek harmony in relationships. The strong respect for authority and controlled or emotionally restrained behaviors of Chinese Americans may translate in the workplace to a genuine loyalty to employers, a desire and willingness to learn from others, internal strength to tolerate crisis situations, and adaptability to change in organizational structure.

- Eighty-three percent of Chinese Americans prefer communications in their native language and speak this language at home.

- The most important holiday is the Chinese New Year or the Spring Festival (*chun jie*).

- Connecting to the market through major organizations and associations is an effective marketing outreach strategy. In addition to professional groups, there are several national advocacy groups that service the needs of the community. Some examples are the Organization of Chinese Americans (OCA) and Chinese American Citizens Alliance (CACA).

A Snapshot: Filipinos

This is the second largest subgroup of the Asian American segment with 2.4 million persons; at least half are women. The population grew 32 percent over the ten-year period from 1990 to 2000. The increase is largely due to immigration as Filipinos led all Asian groups in immigration to the United States.

- Major geographic concentration: Los Angeles (375,000), San Francisco (325,000), Honolulu (180,000).

- The median income of Filipino households is $60,570 vs. $52,616 in median income for all Asian-American households.

- The high income of Filipinos can be attributed to the ongoing stream of highly educated and skilled immigrants from the Philippines and to second- and third-generation Filipino Americans finishing college.

- Psychographics: High rates of acculturation due to English proficiency; heritage, culture and values similar to Hispanics due to 400 year Spanish influence in the Philippine Islands; strong sense of family and community preservation; highly religious, primarily Roman Catholic.

- Family and community dynamics: Filipino Americans come from a society where families, composed of paternal and maternal relatives, are the center of their lives. Its social structure extends to include neighbors, fellow workers, and other community neighbors, called *compadres,* which in Spanish means co-parents or godparents. All of these people are welded together by the *compadrazgo* system, which binds the community together while excluding outsiders. Historically, the *compadrazgo* system created obligations that included sharing food, labor, and financial resources. This system, while religious in origin and designed to assure the protection of the individual through group loyalty, provides a network of associates and contacts which can be leveraged for sales.

- Sixty-six percent of Filipinos prefer to speak their native language at home.

- Filipinos celebrate several events. One in particular is the Lotus Festival where traditional dress and foods are enjoyed. Among the foods are *lumpia* (an egg roll filled with pork, shrimp, and vegetables), *kare* (a peanut-oil-flavored mixture of oxtail and beef tripe), and chicken and pork *adobo* (meat boiled in vinegar, flavored with garlic and spices, and served over rice).

- Among the most well-known national advocacy organizations is the Filipino American National Historical Society. This organization gathers, maintains, and disseminates Filipino-American history.

ASIAN WOMEN LEADING VOICES INTERVIEW

On Challenges in the Retail Process

What I would like companies to know about women of Asian descent is that we have different needs. If it's cosmetics, if it's medical, we always don't have the same kind of reaction to some of the drugs and maybe we only need half of a dose versus an entire dose that a doctor may give. In terms of car companies, because we're shorter—our arms are shorter, our legs are shorter—it makes a little bit of a difference for us when we're sitting in an automobile. As a consumer, if I'm someplace where I don't feel the product or the organization has an understanding of me as a person and, culturally if I feel it's slightly offensive, I won't buy the product. I will leave.

For women in my cultural background, loyalty is also important. If a product seems to work very well, word-of-mouth is key. People tend to be a little more loyal and aren't so apt to just jump around for price. It's about the service and the quality. If something is working well for one person and we talk about it, they're more apt to listen to it and investigate it and see if it would work for them. There's a trust and there's an affinity . . . personal testimonial is the most effective; it's the strongest endorsement of a product.

As an Asian woman to get my business you have to be able to deliver what you say you're going to do . . . pretty straight forward, very simple. If your product performs . . . that's great and if it doesn't I'm going to look someplace else. If you can deliver what you're telling me you're going to do, you've got my business.

A Snapshot: Asian Indians

Asian Indians (2.1 million) are a heterogeneous group, speaking many different languages and coming from a variety of cultural and religious backgrounds. Marketing communications are best executed in English with Indian-national cues woven in for cultural relevance.

- The Asian-Indian population in the U.S. grew 106 percent from 1990 to 2000.

- Major geographic concentration: New York (364,000), San Francisco (143,000), Chicago (124,000).

- The Asian-Indian median household income is $63,669 vs. $52,616 median Asian-American household income.

- Psychographics: National heritage, culture and values are very important; highly price-and-value conscious but very loyal to strong brands; strong emphasis on education—a great percentage of all Asian Americans attend college for a minimum of four years. An example of the strong emphasis on education and professional attainment is in the 38 percent of U.S. medical doctors who are Asian Indian.

- Family and community dynamics: Traditional Asian-Indian family values are highly respected and considered sacred. Modesty is considered a virtue. Many tend to be non-confrontational and accommodating. Asian Indians tend to speak much faster compared with the general public who may have difficulty understanding them. Hindus, who make up 80 percent of the Asian-Indian population traditionally do not eat beef (or any meat) and do not drink alcohol. Second generation Asian Indians who have acculturated into the mainstream will have largely assumed more American values.

- Fifty-five percent of Asian Indians prefer to speak their native language at home.

ASIAN WOMEN LEADING VOICES INTERVIEW

On Challenges in the Workplace

I think the Asian culture has been much more reticent and not as verbal, not as apt to come out and voice opinions or voice it well. From my perspective, I think subtlety is a part of my makeup and when you're working and dealing with the business world, I've had to change that dynamic. I've had to be a little more forceful, but within my range. You have to go toe-to-toe and head-to-head. In some arenas they don't respect you unless you are ... sort of right there with them.

A Snapshot: Korean Americans

The most homogeneous of all Asian groups, the majority of Koreans (1.3 million) have similar economic backgrounds. As immigrants, a high number came to the U.S. as complete family units. Their numbers grew by 35 percent from 1990 to 2000.

- Major geographic concentration: Los Angeles (272,000), New York (168,000), Washington, D.C. (60,000).

- Korean median household income is $40,037 Korean vs. $52,616 median Asian-American household income.

- Psychographics: Strong preference for name brands vs. value brands, independent and assertive; strong emphasis on family and education. Entrepreneurial-driven—33 percent of Korean-American families own small businesses, such as vegetable stands, grocery stores, service stations, and liquor stores. In the 1980s Korean immigrants owned an estimated 95 percent of all dry-cleaning stores in Chicago. By 1990, 15,500 Korean-owned stores were in operation in New York City.

- Family and community dynamics: The family remains very important to Koreans at home and in America. Parents still pressure their children to marry someone who has a good relationship with the family. Children—both male and female—usually are responsible for the care of elderly parents. Tight family bonds continue to exist among Korean Americans. Korean American families often include extended family members. The average Korean-American household consists of more members than the average American family. The 1980 U.S. Census Bureau reported an average of 4.3 members in an Korean-American household, compared with an average of 2.7 persons in a typical American household.

A Snapshot: Vietnamese Americans

Eleven percent of the Asian-American population (1.5 million) is Vietnamese. The population grew 83 percent between 1990 and 2000. A large percentage of Vietnamese originally entered the U.S. as refugees.

- Major geographic concentration: Los Angeles (238,000), San Francisco (156,000), Houston (58,000).

- Vietnamese median household income is $45,085 vs. the $52,616 median Asian-American household income.

- Psychographics: Quality conscious and value seekers; strong political beliefs; strong tendency for cultural and community preservation; family and education are key.

- Family and community dynamics: The extended family is the heart of Vietnamese culture, and preservation of family life is one of the most important concerns of Vietnamese Americans. Older and newly arrived Vietnamese Americans often display indirectness and extreme politeness in dealing with others. They will tend to avoid looking other people in the eyes out of respect, and they frequently try not to express open disagreement with others.

- Vietnamese are well educated and have the highest in-language preference among all Asian groups (93 percent preference for native language).

- The most important Vietnamese holiday is *Tet,* marking both the lunar New Year and the beginning of spring.

A Snapshot: Japanese Americans

Japanese Americans (1.1 million) have the highest numbers of second and third generation Americans. The current population includes acculturated, newly immigrated, students, and intra-company transfers (expatriates).

- Major geographic concentration: Honolulu (215,000), Los Angeles (153,000), and San Francisco (78,000).

- Median household income for Japanese-American households is $52,060 vs. $52,616 median Asian-American household income.

- Psychographics: Value consensus over individual opinion—a collectivist point of view; value name brands over price brands; strong family values; strong emphasis on education and accomplishment; prestige is key.

- Family and community dynamics: As with other Asian cultures, the family represents the central nucleus in the Japanese community. Elders and ancestors are highly respected and valued and the concept of family extends beyond the traditional father-mother-children bond to include cousins, aunts, uncles, and others. Men play a more dominant role in decision making, although with the strong emphasis of second- and third- generation Japanese Americans in this country, the influence of women has grown and continues to drive product selection.

THINK ABOUT IT

Asian-American women are an untapped market segment. Once you have CEO and senior level commitment, what other strategies can you employ to reach Asian-American women?

- Determine whether enhancements to your products and services are required to better meet the customer needs of Asian Americans.

- Analyze your communications toolbox—website, print media, broadcast, catalog—to make sure you market your products in the preferred language of your target audience.

- Identify the major Asian-American events that are taking place in your market. Attend, participate, network.

- Involve yourself and your teams in the local media. Use bi-lingual skills, if applicable, to connect with the media and local press.

- Know the Asian-American small business owners in the areas where your products and services are sold. Target marketing efforts to these highly networked businesses.

continues . . .

- Explore the referral energy of your existing Asian-American customer and distributor base to identify more prospects.

- Customize your existing referral strategy to ensure it is culturally relevant to the target audience.

- Align your corporate efforts with major organizations and advocacy groups that support the Asian-American community.

- Build third-party credibility.

- Educate yourself about the market. Continue to develop cultural competency.

PART THREE

The Intersection of Gender, Diversity, and Lifestage

SEVEN

Mothers of Color

LET'S TURN OUR ATTENTION now to better understanding how culture and ethnicity intersect with gender and life stage. More specifically, this chapter will focus on the unique dynamics, size, trends, and issues mothers of color experience as they form and raise families.

Marketing teams are already faced with recession challenges and an increasingly consumer-controlled media marketplace. They now need to focus on the fact that the quintessential consumer audience that makes decisions not only for herself, but for her family members—mothers—is comprised largely of ethnic women who may speak a different language, have larger households, be single heads of households, and work two or more jobs. Marketers need to come to grips with the fact that although 35 percent of all women in the U.S. are multicultural, *almost half—46 percent—of all mothers are Latina, Black, or Asian.* This has a direct and proportional impact on how and where marketing strategies should be targeted. Needless to say, it also impacts how budgets should be spent. Therefore, companies whose products are for children, or who rely on mothers as the primary purchaser, will benefit from including insights from mothers of color in their overall marketing strategies to grow market share, optimize brand performance, and re-invigorate their businesses.

Who are these mothers? How large is this audience? How much economic power do they have? How different are their needs relative to mothers in general? How can you best reach and persuade them to consider your brands? And, what about the children of these women?

129

What are some of the important insights you need to consider in marketing to families of color?

All moms are not created equal

Let's begin with the basics. All moms are *not* created equal! We've already established through the U.S. Census Bureau that 46 percent of all mothers in this country are Latina, Black, or Asian. Among women in general, 67 percent of all women of color aged 15 to 44 are mothers compared with 55 percent of all women aged 15 to 44 who are mothers. Whether or not marketers realize it, these women are making several purchase decisions on a daily basis about the products and services they will consider and buy for themselves and for their families. This audience has a disproportionately higher impact on the success of a company's brand than their population size would naturally warrant.

By cultural group, the highest representation of mothers of color is among Latinas. Among women aged 15 to 44, *73 percent* of Hispanic women are mothers; *62 percent* of African-American women are mothers; and, *60 percent* of Asian women are mothers. In every instance, women of color experience a higher incidence of motherhood than Caucasian women.

Mothers of color spend $620 billion annually

Based on what is estimated to be a $1.6 trillion mother's economic market, mothers of color generate $620 billion, or 40 percent of the total spending done by women with children under age 18. This 620 billion dollars will grow to nearly one trillion dollars by 2020—a little more than a decade.

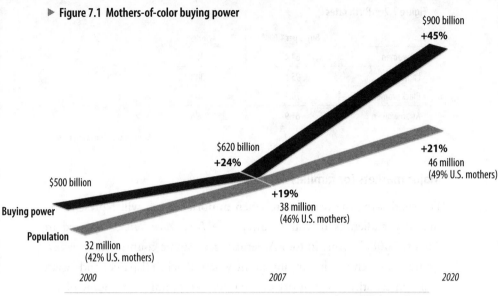

▶ Figure 7.1 Mothers-of-color buying power

$900 billion
+45%

$620 billion
+24%

+21%
46 million
(49% U.S. mothers)

$500 billion

Buying power

+19%
38 million
(46% U.S. mothers)

Population

32 million
(42% U.S. mothers)

2000   2007   2020

Source: U.S. Census Bureau

Children of color lead the way

According to analyses of U.S. census data released in August of 2008, racial and ethnic minorities account for 44 percent of all individuals under age 20. Moreover, 48 percent of all births in the U.S. in the last year were multicultural infants. By 2023, the majority of all children under age 18 will be Latino, Black, or Asian American. And by 2050, 62 percent of all children in this country will be of "minority" origin. We have larger households—on average at least one to two persons more per household than Caucasian households—and we have large extended families that are central to the survival of our everyday lives.

Births to Hispanic women in the United States exceeded 1 million for the first time in 2005. Therefore, of the 4 million children born in the U.S. on an annual basis, approximately 25 percent are of Hispanic ancestry. Latinas also have the highest birth rate at 95.4 births per thousand, which is 48 percent higher the birth rate of all women. Birth rates among Black women are the second highest at 70.2 per thousand, and the Asian birth rate is slightly lower than women overall at 61.9 per thousand.

> By 2023, the majority of all U.S. children under age 18 will be Latino, Black, or Asian American.

▶ Figure 7.2   Birth rates

	Births per 1,000	Index
All women	64.4	100
Latinas	95.4	148
Black women	70.2	109
Asian women	61.9	96

Source: U.S. Census Bureau

Major markets for families of color

Foreshadowing the near future when minority youth will represent the majority audiences in this country, *The New York Times* reported in August 2008, "...one in four American geographic counties have passed or are approaching the tipping point where Black, Hispanic, and Asian children constitute a majority of the under 20 population." Some of the states where there are large numbers of families of color include: California, Texas, New Mexico, Arizona and Nevada. The Northeast coast is giving way to an older Caucasian demographic, where many families are childless, empty nesters. The good news is that diverse families of color are filling this gap in the Northeast and represent a gold mine of current and future customers for brands across a variety of industries including apparel, toiletries, food, beverage, educational products, new technology, cell phones, financial products, insurance, college education savings programs, music, and toys.

▶ Figure 7.3   Family diversity by geographic region, 2007

percent of families by race, with teenagers aged 12 to 17

	White, non-Hispanic	Hispanic	Black	Asian	Total
Northeast	66%	14%	16%	4%	100%
Midwest	77	6	14	3	100
South	58	16	23	3	100
West	51	31	7	11	100

Source: U.S. Census Bureau

Mothers-of-color insights

The mothers who are making the primary product decisions for these majority "minority" children represent an important pipeline of current and future business. Many are first-time parents, very anxious and concerned about "getting it right," and making the perfect decision for their new families. Those who are immigrants want to take advantage of the many new products that are available for the healthy development of their infants—but they need help in making the right choices. Like other parents, they want only the best they can afford for their growing families. Recognizing the trepidation many of these new mothers will experience, marketers have the opportunity to provide information, gain trust, and instill confidence in their products and services to this $620 billion consumer segment. Done correctly, with communication, product, promotional, key influencer endorsements, and sales strategies that reflect knowledge of what motivates mothers of color to purchase and what influences their decisions will result in strong referrals and word-of-mouth endorsement to friends and family for years to come.

INSIGHT #1   THE BEAUTY OF MOTHERHOOD

Attitudinally, women of color place a higher regard on motherhood than other groups. Specifically, according to a study done by Yankelovich, Latina and African American women are more likely to state that, "having a child is an experience every woman should have." Seventy-four percent of Hispanic women agree with this statement, compared with 57 percent of African-American women and 49 percent of non-Hispanic White women. Data for Asian mothers was not reported, although interviews conducted for this book would support the importance of motherhood among Asian women, as well. Marketers can leverage this insight in their business plans by celebrating "family" as a positive and natural outgrowth of the cultural values of mothers of color and making sure that promotions geared to mothers include a representative range of children of color of all heritages, among other strategies. Just as it is important to see women-of-color images reflected in beauty, fashion, and cosmetic marketing strategies, it is important to reflect credible and honest images of children of color in targeted communications, as well.

INSIGHT #2   MULTI-TASKING IS THE NORM

Most mothers of color are "working mothers." U.S. Census figures show that married African-American mothers with children under age 18 have higher rates of workforce participation than other married mothers—82 percent compared with 55 percent of White moms, 66 percent of Asian moms, and 62 percent of Hispanic moms. It's important to note that women of color have *always* worked and *always* raised families—sometimes raising more than one family. Women of color have not had the luxury of being stay-at-home mothers. For pure economic reasons they have always had to juggle multiple responsibilities, sometimes never finding that happy "work life balance" women seek today. The very concept of multi-tasking was likely invented—and has certainly been mastered—by mothers of color.

The implication for marketers is that mothers of color are time-pressed and time-poor—even more so than Caucasian mothers. Therefore, the initial point of brand interaction with mothers of color must have impact, be clearly differentiated, and be sustainable over time. They are more risk averse and prefer the "tried and true" methods versus something new. And, if they venture out to experiment with a new product or service, their expectations will be extremely high. As one mother-of-color reported: "If I find a product that really speaks to my needs, I tend to stick with that product. If I have a good thing, I continue to stay with it and I share it with my friends because I want them to know how I feel about that product...." And, "If a company does not meet my style, my tendency is that I sever the ties...I don't go back. I don't have time to play."

The stresses of multi-tasking also lead mothers to search for ways to reward themselves. As such, the "little indulgences," the "affordable luxuries"—such as getting a manicure, having one's hair done, or relaxing with a glass of wine with friends—make a huge difference in the lives of mothers of color. One executive mother-of-color expressed this need in this way: "On the surface we are the same, but how we live and what we need to accomplish for our families on a day-to-day basis is very stressful [from mainstream mothers]. So the mindset is different . . . companies don't get that, because they live in a very insulated world." To the extent that marketers can surround their brands with promotions that offer "indulgent escapes" and allow mothers of color to momentarily press the "pause button" in their lives, they will be rewarded with their loyalty and business.

INSIGHT #3   MOTHERS ARE UNDER THE MICROSCOPE AT WORK

The higher labor force participation rate of mothers of color versus mainstream working mothers results in greater stress and a never-ending search for the most convenient, inexpensive, and safest way to care for children who are at home. A mother-of-color feels the economic need to work and to perform exceptionally well on the job: no absences, on time attendance, superior work, and consistent results. She may be reluctant to take advantage of the work-life flexibility benefits offered at her job for fear of being viewed as "someone who needs special attention." This was the sentiment of several individuals interviewed for this book. Respondents felt that a mother-of-color had to be extremely cautious about leaving work early to attend a school event or staying home with a sick child. The idea of being on the "mommy track" and spending the formative years with infants at home is a luxury many mothers of color believe they cannot afford, for fear that when they return to work their hard-fought position as manager may not be there waiting for them. The implication for businesses that seek to recruit and retain a more diverse workforce is that they may need to over-communicate and consistently reinforce their commitment to work-life flexibility to reduce the anxiety women of color may feel on the job.

At home, a mother-of-color will delegate more responsibility to her children in the form of household chores and taking care of children in the family, and do so at an earlier age than mainstream mothers may consider appropriate. Some of this behavior is the result of marital status: 70 percent of Black babies are born to single mothers; 52 percent of Latino babies have no fathers present. Great-grandmothers are bringing up little children. According to the National Center for Health Statistics, 22 percent of White children live with no man in the household; by contrast 31 percent of Hispanic children and 56 percent of Black children live in a household where no man is present. Mothers heading these households need their children to be independent and capable of caring for themselves at as early an age as possible.

The tendency to raise independent children at an earlier age is also due to the belief that many mothers of color have about the need to prepare their children for the harsh realities of the world. Black and Hispanic mothers, in particular, feel that the perils for children of color are greater—especially children who are unprepared. Therefore, these mothers are vigilant about ensuring their children receive the necessary skills to overcome challenges that will inevitably be presented—whether in school, in the neighborhood, on the job, or in unfamiliar surroundings. These survival skills are taught early and come in the form of strict discipline and adherence to rules that are set in the household by both parents. Contrary to mainstream values, which encourage self-expression, freethinking, and challenging the norm—sometimes including authority figures—among young children, mothers- (and fathers-) of-color tend to be disciplinarians. The implication for marketers is that the child-parent dynamic between mothers of color and their children is unique and centered in the goal of raising strong, independent and self-reliant young adults. Products and services that assist in fulfilling this objective will be welcomed by mothers of color.

INSIGHT #5   A SOURCE OF INSPIRATION

Despite the challenges of motherhood, mothers of color are an important catalyst for creating prosperity and giving back economic resources and support within their communities. Not only do they spend billions of dollars in goods and services, but they also inspire giving in the community. "Within churches," as one executive interviewed for this book shared, "there are all men at the pulpit, but the mothers are tithing . . . the mothers are making sure the faith values are being instilled in the children . . . the mothers are serving and leading the way for others as an example." It is no wonder that faith-based organizations represent an important pathway to reach mothers of color and that communities of color thrive by targeting mothers of color.

INSIGHT #6   THE MULTICULTURAL "SANDWICH" GENERATION

While more and more baby boomers are waking up to the fact that they will need to care for their aging parents, "boomers of color" have always accepted this as a cultural reality. Care for parents of multicultural families has more often been provided in the home versus in a nursing or elder care facility. The expectation of family elder care is a reality and one that, frankly, will grow over time in proportion to the growth in population of elder persons of color. Marketers have an opportunity to build relationships with these audiences today for the future business they will represent. However, before they take this step marketers need to understand how mothers of color, the principal caretakers of parents, view elder care.

In communities of color, culture and tradition require that children take personal responsibility for the physical and financial care of their parents. The idea of placing one's parent in a nursing home is, for the most part, unthinkable. Marketers can, through ethnographic research and consumer studies, better understand the cultural tension consumers of color have with the issue of mainstream elder care and traditional cultural values. Through this process they can identify ways to reassure this multicultural sandwich generation of 'best in class' services for their parents, without creating unnecessary guilt and further tension. The business potential associated in leveraging diversity elder care is large. Using the mainstream market as a proxy, the AARP reported that over 41 percent of all baby boomers with a living parent provided a total of $350 billion in some form of financial or personal aid for their care in 2006.

INSIGHT #7   RISK AVERSION

The stresses and challenges of raising more children than your White female counterparts, not always having the economic resources to hire help to clean, cook, and care for the children, the absence, in large part, of a partner to help raise your family, the lack of "me" time, caring for parents, and the real and perceived challenges of the workplace all add to more risk-averse behavior among mothers of color than among their female Caucasian counterparts. They are skeptical of untried, untested, un-endorsed products. You have to work harder to win their loyalty, and to give them the assurance that your products and services are worth their attention.

One way to ensure the risk-averse needs of mothers of color are addressed is through a strong customer service and follow-through strategy—one that provides assurance that their decisions are the right decisions. Strategies that reinforce a money-back guarantee, safety, testimonials from other customers, third-party endorsements, service warranties, and customer hotline support all work together to relieve the anxiety and stress of these parents. Couple this with a sales strategy that trains those in the front line—sales and service representatives—on how to interact with mothers of color in a way that is respectful of their time, acknowledges their desire for proof that your product will work, and follows up with an appreciative "thank you for your business," and you will be ahead of your competition in gaining market share with this majority audience.

So, what does the future of mothers of color look like?

The future is very promising and lucrative from a mother-of-color per-spective. Based on population growth trends, the percentage of moth-ers-of-color in this country will grow from the current 46 percent level to 49 percent by 2020, to 56 percent by 2030 and to 66 percent by 2050. *Importantly, in states like California, over 70 percent of all mothers today are mothers of color.* "If we want to see what the future of Cali-fornia looks like, we just have to go to the delivery room," said David Hayes-Bautista, a professor of medicine and director of the Center for the Study of Latino Health and Culture at UCLA. "In 2016, the babies born in 1998 will be eligible to vote. Half of those new votes will be Latino."

Virtually any marketer across a wide spectrum of products and ser-vices has an opportunity to grow market share by focusing on mothers of color as a key target.

THINK ABOUT IT

There is tremendous diversity in the mothers-and-children market. Within 20 years, the majority of all U.S. children under age 18 will be Latino, Black, or Asian American.

Product implications

How are you adapting your product lines in the toy, technology, fashion, clothing, music, educational, food and beverage industries to address the preferences of these young customers? How are you engaging their mothers in the purchase consideration?

Almost half of all mothers today are mothers of color.

These women control the spending decisions in their households. How much of their business are you leaving on the table by not courting them as consumers?

Mothers of color control $620 billion in spending—$900 billion by 2020

What is your current budget allocation to the mothers market? How much of this budget is directed to Latina, Black, and Asian mothers? What can you do today to create a "right-sized" budget plan?

EIGHT

Entrepreneurial Women of Power

IT'S A FACT: businesses owned by women of color constitute the *fastest growing segment* of the U.S. economy. They are starting businesses at five times the rate of all businesses in the U.S. and for the past twenty years, businesses owned by Asians, Hispanics, African Americans, Native Americans, and other Pacific Islanders have outpaced the growth rate of *all* firms in the United States. It's clear that women-of-color entrepreneurs are becoming accepted as an important part of the business community. It's also vitally important for companies to reach out to budding and successful entrepreneurs as prospective suppliers for your business, customers of your products, and ambassadors of your brand for the influential leverage that they represent in their communities.

In 2006, according to the Small Business Administration (SBA) Office of Advocacy, there were 1.9 million firms in the United States with majority ownership by women of color. These firms employ 1.2 million people and generate $165 billion annually in gross sales receipts. As a whole, women of color comprise approximately one-quarter of all women-owned firms.

Revenue growth for women-of-color-owned companies—a good sign of momentum—is moving at a rate faster than start-ups. Between 2002 and 2008, the number of women-of-color entrepreneurs grew by 32 percent and revenues increased by 48 percent. Employment by women-of-color firms was also up by 27 percent during this time period. Therefore, these women are making serious investments in their businesses for long-term growth. Entrepreneurial women of color are providing much needed economic vitality to the U.S. GDP as well as to the communities in which their businesses are located.

Why you should care about women-of-color entrepreneurs

Women-of-color-owned businesses constitute the fastest growing segment of the U.S. economy.

Beyond the fact that women-of-color entrepreneurs, along with women business owners in general, create jobs in our communities for millions of people, these women are attractive from a marketing perspective. They represent a highly motivated, highly connected, intelligent, and influential set of leaders, customers, and suppliers for your products and services.

- **Highly motivated and networked audience.** Women business owners and women-of-color entrepreneurs are a highly "charged" group of women who understand that they must work together to succeed. They are members of various professional, women's, and industry groups and work hard to meet new people in their field that will further their businesses. They recognize networking as an essential ingredient to success and they are quick to recommend another company, brand, service, and prospect if they believe you offer value.

- **Influential in the community.** Women-of-color entrepreneurs can serve as powerful role models and third-party direct endorsers of your products and services. Because they are leaders in the community, they are often in the press, attend local events, and seek ways to stay connected to local market activities. An association with your brand can result in positive media and stronger consideration among prospective buyers.

- **Suppliers of your goods.** Driving diversity from a supplier perspective makes good business sense. It is an effective way to ensure that you are providing economic stimulus to the communities where your products are purchased. In addition, all things being equal, ethnic consumers prefer to purchase products from companies that give back to their communities. By promoting your association with women-of-color entrepreneurs, whose business services encompass a variety of industry sectors, you are increasing the likelihood of positive brand consideration in the women-of-color markets.

- **Geographic reach and employee customer pool.** Women-of-color entrepreneurs have businesses across major markets in the U.S. and provide broad access in high opportunity markets. Their employees—millions of individuals—represent potential customers of your products. Properly marketed to, with the support and influence of the company owners, these employees represent added business for your products and services.

- **Youthful.** As mentioned earlier, we know that women of color are an average *eleven years younger* than non-Hispanic White females. The median age is 31 years compared with 42 years for U.S. females overall. With these additional eleven years comes the opportunity to generate more sales over the lifetime of the customer. The same is true among women-of-color entrepreneurs. According to the U.S. Economic Census, majority women-of-color business owners tend to be younger than their mainstream counterparts. Properly supported, this youthfulness can translate to a longer lifetime business opportunity than with other supplier and customer groups.

A snapshot of Latina-owned businesses

The U.S. Bureau of Labor Statistics reported that in 2002, there were 540,745 majority-owned Latina firms plus an additional 111,536 firms equally owned by both Latinas and Latinos for a total of 652,281. Therefore, a Latina, either as the majority or equal owner, owns 41 percent of all Latino-owned companies in the United States. Although less than 10 percent of these Latina-owned firms have paid employees, those who do have paid employees have an average of 6.7 employees per firm, a figure comparable to their Latino male counterparts at 8 employees per firm.

From a revenue perspective, Latina business owners generated gross sales receipts of $53.9 billion, or 24 percent of total sales for all Hispanic-owned firms. This is less than their fair share of the number of Latino firms owned at 41 percent. The average revenue per Latina-owned company was $82,000. However, the average revenue per Latina-owned company *with employees* was significantly higher at $645,515. This demonstrates the financial results of investing in a solid company strategy and having an employee team to support business objectives. By comparison, the average revenue per Latino-male-owned company (majority and equally owned) was approximately $180,700; those with employees generated $891,854. Latina entrepreneurs with employees generated 72 percent of what their male counterparts did during 2002. While still a disparity in earnings, this is ahead of the pay inequities we see in the workforce among Latinas and men (52 cents earned by a Latina for every dollar earned by a non-Hispanic White male).

Culturally, Latina entrepreneurs are passionate about their businesses and about their successes. They are determined, like other women business owners, to go the distance and to take matters into their own hands to make success possible. Where they differ from their mainstream female counterparts is in their motivation to succeed. Many times their motivation is driven by personal situations. In some cases, they are single parents, recent arrivals to this country, or sole providers in the household. Regardless of the circumstance, the realization of the "American Dream" is an important goal for many Hispanic women and one that is obtainable through hard work and commitment. The success stories of other Latinas who have made their mark by owning their own companies, the strong networking skills of Latinas especially with other Latinas, and the tendency to nurture others go a long way in creating pathways of success for Hispanic women. Latina majority owned businesses are a powerful statement of success to the community-at-large.

▶ **Figure 8.1   Snapshot of businesses owned by Hispanics**

	Number of firms	Rcpts ($000s)	Number of employer firms	Rcpts for employers ($000s)	Number of employees	Annual payroll ($000s)
All Latino	1,573,464	221,927,425	199,542	179,507,959	1,536,795	36,711,718
Majority Female-owned	540,745	35,265,399	43,142	25,726,727	282,683	6,182,203
Male-owned	921,183	168,061,827	136,832	139,486,041	1,113,277	27,852,670
Equally male-/ female-owned	111,536	18,600,200	19,568	14,295,191	140,835	2,676,846

Source: U.S. Bureau of Labor Statistics, 2002

Top ten states for majority Latina-owned businesses

California, Texas, Florida, New York, New Jersey, Illinois, Arizona, New Mexico, Colorado, and Massachusetts represent the top ten states for Latina majority-owned businesses. They account for 87 percent of all Hispanic women majority owned companies and 82 percent ($29 billion) of all gross sales receipts nationwide.

▶ **Figure 8.2   Latina-owned firms by geography**

	Latina majority owned firms	Rcpts ($000s)	Number of employer firms	Rcpts for employers ($000s)	Number of employees
California	154,869	9,923,952	10,438	6,962,741	67,661
Texas	91,606	4,900,783	6,623	3,330,548	60,292
Florida	81,553	5,554,444	8,548	4,213,541	40,917
New York	72,986	2,897,516	3,151	1,790,663	15,598
New Jersey	18,001	1,465,444	1,780	1,166,693	8,929
Illinois	12,910	1,355,662	1,378	1,118,863	12,965
Arizona	12,389	876,158	1,183	615,254	7,108
New Mexico	10,769	813,315	976	647,219	7,282
Colorado	9,541	622,111	920	446,715	7,049
Massachusetts	6,499	561,711	510	441,450	5,847

Source: U.S. Bureau of Labor Statistics, 2002

Major industry sectors

The retail and wholesale industries account for approximately $10 billion in revenue generated by majority owned Latina firms. They constitute the largest percentage of business at 31 percent. Health care and social service assistance, administrative support and accommodations, and food services represent an additional 25 percent ($8.9 billion), while manufacturing and construction account for approximately 15 percent of revenue ($5.7 billion).

▶ Figure 8.3   Latina majority businesses, by industry revenue mix, 2002

Health care and social assistance	10%
Retail trade	17
Administrative & support/waste management	9
Arts, entertainment, recreation	1
Accommodation, food services	6
Finance and insurance	3
Information	0
Manufacturing	8
Other services (except public administration)	7
Professional, scientific & technical services	9
Real estate, rental, leasing	4
Educational services	0
Transportation, warehousing	2
Construction	8
Wholesale trade	14
Other services	2
Total	100

Source: U.S. Bureau of Labor Statistics, 2002

A snapshot of Black women-owned businesses

During 2002 the U.S. Census Bureau reported that there were 547,032 African-American majority women-owned firms plus an additional 79,034 firms equally owned by both Black men and women for a total of 626,066. Therefore, a Black woman, either as the majority or equal owner, owns 52 percent of all Black-owned companies in the U.S.—higher than her Latina counterpart at 41 percent. Although only 5.8 percent of these Black-women-owned firms have paid employees, those that do employ an average of 7.2 individuals per firm, a figure slighter higher than for Latina business owners, and lower than their Black male counterparts at 8.6 employees per firm.

From a revenue perspective, Black women business owners generated gross sales receipts of $27.1 billion, or 31 percent of total sales for all Black-owned firms. This is less than their fair share of the number of Black firms owned at 52 percent, suggesting lower productivity. This is, in fact the case. The average revenue generated per Black-woman-owned company was $43,000—nearly half of the gross receipts per company generated by Latina entrepreneurs and $61,500 less than the average revenues generated by Black male-owned businesses (both majority and equally owned firms) at $104,500. When looking at the average revenue generated by Black-female-owned firms *with employees* the figure was significantly higher at $482,284. By comparison, the average revenue per Black-male-owned company with employees (majority and equally owned) was higher yet at $782,674. Black women business owners with employees generated only 62 percent of what their male counterparts did in revenues during 2002.

This inequity in revenue is in contrast to the gains Black women have made in the workplace. This suggests that Black men are more successful *outside* the corporate setting in charting their ascent up the corporate ladder, being their own bosses, and spearheading their own economic futures. This can also suggest that Black female entrepreneurs have significant hurdles to overcome in an unstructured business environment where mentors, access to capital, economic resources, and business-planning support are not readily available. Corporations willing to invest in the longer-term potential of Black female business owners will want to collaborate with research organizations such as the National Center for Women's Business Research, the National Association of Women Business Owners (NAWBO), The Links, Inc., and other women's business advocacy groups to identify the reasons for this inequity and create an action plan for turnaround results.

▶ Figure 8.4   Snapshot of businesses owned by African-Americans

	Number of firms	Rcpts ($000s)	Number of employer firms	Rcpts for employers ($000s)	Number of employees	Annual payroll ($000s)
All Black	1,197,567	88,641,608	94,518	65,799,425	753,978	17,550,064
Majority Female-owned	547,032	20,670,616	27,027	12,975,918	176,436	3,911,432
Male-owned	571,501	61,562,301	58,054	48,213,424	492,341	12,173,348
Equally male-/ female-owned	79,034	6,408,691	9,437	4,610,083	85,201	1,465,284

Source: U.S. Census Economic Labor Statistics, 2002

Top ten states for majority Black women-owned businesses

New York, California, Florida, Georgia, Illinois, Texas, Maryland, Michigan, North Carolina, and Ohio represent the top ten states for businesses majority owned by Black women. They account for 59 percent of all Black majority women-owned companies and 51 percent ($13.7 billion) of all gross sales receipts nationwide.

▶ Figure 8.5   Businesses owned by Black women, geographically

	Black female majority owned businesses	Rcpts ($000s)	Number of employer firms	Rcpts for employers ($000s)	Number of employees
New York	62,313	1,491,392	1,780	610,241	8,597
California	52,651	2,942,376	2,648	2,153,259	15,310
Florida	46,493	1,257,665	1,924	549,544	10,344
Georgia	41,276	1,299,683	1,760	647,714	8,433
Illinois	39,766	1,626,990	1,400	1,127,507	11,978
Texas	34,488	1,524,555	2,002	1,011,827	21,484
Maryland	31,955	1,358,390	1,322	836,504	9,916
Michigan	23,796	865,118	1,046	561,963	7,091
North Carolina	21,563	670,096	1,399	415,635	9,328
Ohio	17,561	650,407	901	398,096	5,545

Source: U.S. Bureau of Labor Statistics, 2002

Major industry sectors

The health care and social services industry represent the lion's share of revenue generated by Black women majority owned businesses at $5.3 billion or 25.6 percent of total gross sales receipts, followed by professional, scientific and technical services at 11.6 percent ($2.4 billion). In addition, retail trade represents a $1.8 billion business segment among Black women entrepreneurs, generating an 8.7 percent contribution to total revenue.

▶ Figure 8.6   Black women majority business owners, by industry, 2002

Industry	% of revenue
Health care and social assistance	25%
Retail trade	9
Administrative & support/waste management	8
Arts, entertainment, recreation	3
Accommodation, food services	4
Finance and insurance	3
Information	0
Manufacturing	3
Other services (except public administration)	10
Professional, scientific & technical services	11
Real estate, rental, leasing	4
Educational services	2
Transportation, warehousing	3
Construction	6
Wholesale trade	9
Other services	0
Total *(May not add to 100 percent due to rounding)*	100

Source: U.S. Bureau of Labor Statistics, 2002

A snapshot of Asian women-owned businesses

Without question, the most successful of all female business owners are Asian women. In 2002, the U.S. Bureau of Labor Statistics reported that there were 339,554 majority-female-owned Asian firms plus an additional 123,670 firms equally owned by both Asian men and women for a total of 463,224. Asian women, either as the majority or equal owner, own 42 percent of all Asian businesses in the United States. Twenty-five percent of Asian women business owners have employees, a figure higher than any other woman-of-color entrepreneurial segment. They employ an average of 6.3 employees per firm, a figure comparable to Black business women (at 6.7 employees per firm), and slightly below their Asian male counterparts at 7.2 employees per firm.

Dollar to dollar, Asian Americans are transacting more business than any other group. They have the highest percent of business owners among all minorities. Nearly 6 percent of all U.S. business owners are Asian compared with their population share at 4.4 percent. Asian's high entrepreneurship rate has accelerated Asian business growth. As reported in *USA Today*, there are 10,600 Asian companies in the U.S. for every 100,000 Asian adults—nearly twice the rate for Hispanics and African-Americans.

From a revenue perspective, Asian-women-business owners generated gross sales receipts of $92.2 billion, or 28 percent of total sales for all Asian-owned firms. This is less than their fair share of the number of Asian firms owned at 42 percent. However, this $92.2 billion is more than the gross sales receipt of Latina and Black women business owners combined.

Average revenue per Asian-woman-owned business was nearly $200,000 in 2002. This far exceeds average revenue of other women of color and of both Latino men and Black business owners. Asian men generated $764,033 in average revenue per firm—both majority and equal owned firms. Among those Asian female entrepreneurs with employees, the average revenue was $674,000—comparable to earnings among Latina entrepreneurs with employees (4.4 percent higher), but dramatically higher than Black female entrepreneurs with employees (39.8 percent). Asian male entrepreneurs with employees generated an average revenue stream of nearly one million dollars ($991,588) in 2002.

▶ Figure 8.7   Snapshot of Asian-owned businesses

	Number of firms	Rcpts ($000s)	Number of employer firms	Rcpts for employers ($000s)	Number of employees	Annual payroll ($000s)
All Asian	1,103,587	326,663,445	319,468	291,162,771	2,213,948	56,044,960
Majority Female-owned	339,554	53,652,929	71,177	44,960,347	425,024	9,957,511
Male-owned	640,363	234,428,718	203,504	213,000,919	1,485,834	40,531,219
Equally male-/ female-owned	123,670	38,581,797	44,787	33,201,506	303,089	5,556,230

Source: U.S. Bureau of Labor Statistics, 2002

Top ten states for majority Asian women-owned businesses

California, New York, Texas, Hawaii, New Jersey, Florida, Illinois, Virginia, Washington, D.C., and Georgia represent the top ten states for businesses majority owned by Asian women. They account for 78 percent of all Asian majority women business owned companies and 80 percent ($42.8 billion) of all gross sales receipts nationwide.

▶ Figure 8.8   Asian women-owned businesses, geographically

	Asian female majority owned businesses	Rcpts ($000s)	Number of employer firms	Rcpts for employers ($000s)	Number of employees
California	118,527	21,582,901	24,720	18,259,646	140,605
New York	39,756	4,471,181	6,332	3,600,341	32,564
Texas	25,346	3,688,756	5,080	3,045,403	52,770
Hawaii	14,896	2,144,121	2,371	1,794,133	18,011
New Jersey	14,521	2,873,056	3,538	2,458,887	15,517
Florida	12,860	2,108,534	3,140	1,762,041	21,020
Illinois	12,360	2,088,226	2,466	1,776,520	13,332
Virginia	9,661	1,452,027	2,060	1,251,502	14,204
Washington	9,020	1,159,229	2,047	970,093	8,412
Georgia	8,682	1,276,983	1,754	999,437	8,010

Source: U.S. Bureau of Labor Statistics, 2002

Major industry sectors

A full 44 percent of all revenue generated among majority Asian women business owners is concentrated in the retail and wholesale trade sectors. Over $23 billion was generated through this industry sector in 2002. Health care and social services plus accommodation services represented an additional 23 percent of total ($12.4 billion). Manufacturing represents a $3 billion source of business for Asian women majority business owners (5.7 percent of total).

▶ **Figure 8.9   Asian women business owners, revenue by industry, 2002**

Industry	% of revenue
Health care and social assistance	13%
Retail trade	20
Administrative & support/waste management	2
Arts, entertainment, recreation	1
Accommodation, food services	11
Finance and insurance	2
Information	3
Manufacturing	6
Other services (except public administration)	10
Professional, scientific & technical services	9
Real estate, rental, leasing	3
Educational services	2
Transportation, warehousing	1
Construction	3
Wholesale trade	23
Other services	1
Total *(May not add to 100 percent due to rounding)*	100

Source: U.S. Bureau of Labor Statistics, 2002

Other women-of-color-owned business snapshots
American Indian, Alaska Native, Native Hawaiian, Other Asian Pacific Islander

Among other businesswomen of color, American Indian and Native Alaskan women account for 42 percent of all entrepreneurs within their ethnic and cultural segments, and generate over $6 billion in gross sales receipts. They employ over 50,000 persons. Those who have employees generate an average of $583,249 per firm. Their male counterparts who are majority business owners generate an average of $878,400 per firm.

Among Native Hawaiian and other Pacific Islanders, there are 12.8 million women business owners, or 44 percent of all businesses represented by this cultural and ethnic group. They generate $620 million in gross revenue sales and employ over 7,000 employees. Average revenue per woman-owned firm is estimated at approximately $50,000 compared with an average of $177,000 among their male counterparts.

▶ Figure 8.10   Snapshot of businesses owned by American Indian and Alaska natives

American Indian & Alaska Native	Number of firms	Rcpts ($000s)	Number of employer firms	Rcpts for employers ($000s)	Number of employees	Annual pay-roll ($000s)
All firms	201,387	26,872,947	24,498	21,986,696	191,270	5,135,273
Majority Female-owned	78,292	5,763,268	7,372	4,409,219	49,406	1,102,515
Male-owned	116,408	17,734,650	15,939	14,391,110	119,239	3,222,438
Equally male-/ female-owned	6,477	649,530	980	462,077	5,565	99,846

Source: U.S. Bureau of Labor Statistics

▶ Figure 8.11   Snapshot of businesses owned by Native Hawaiian and other Pacific Islanders

Native Hawaiian and other Pacific Islander	Number of firms	Rcpts ($000s)	Number of employer firms	Rcpts for employers ($000s)	Number of employees	Annual pay-roll ($000s)
All firms	28,948	4,279,591	3,693	3,502,157	29,319	826,217
Female-owned	10,582	795,963	837	620,578	7,395	148,814
Male-owned	16,178	3,262,888	2,690	2,786,672	20,421	653,316
Equally male-/ female-owned	2,188	220,739	N/A	N/A	N/A	N/A

Source: U.S. Bureau of Labor Statistics, 2002

Underlying dynamics of growth

Why are so many of us rushing to hang out an "open for business" sign? What are some of the underlying dynamics that stimulate so many women, and women of color in particular, in the move towards micro enterprise? Some of the reasons that drive the passion of being an entrepreneur are greater control of one's future, improved economic status, control over one's time and flexibility with work-family balance, and personal and professional self-actualization.

Other reasons why we're seeing a huge surge of women shifting into the business ownership sector are related to dissatisfaction with the corporate setting, frustration over the "glass ceiling" effect, and systematic pay inequities. Although corporations have taken quantum leaps forward in working to build inclusive workplaces and expand opportunities for women and business, women of color still earn less than White men and women with similar education and job descriptions. While there are financial challenges to being an entrepreneur, there also is a greater sense that "the sky is the limit" and that one is only limited by the extent of one's hard work and creativity. Some women feel that they are being pushed out the corporate door while they still have tremendous energy, talent, and unused skills that can result in a meaningful business proposition. One research respondent summed up the frustration of not being fully used in the workforce as follows:

> "I want [corporate America] . . . to let me into the inner circles and to mentor me—especially along the choppy waters of politics. . . . if they don't understand that, then they risk losing me. And frankly, with women representing half the population and effectively half the (potential) workforce, what will happen is eventually companies will come to a point where they'll be struggling to attract female talent because we'll have learned to work without them."

Entrepreneurship also serves a practical purpose in helping to bridge the economic gap that many pre-retirees find themselves when they insufficient resources to comfortably retire. A new business start up that requires little up front capital, low overhead, and leverages years of experience in a business environment represents an ideal fit for these individuals.

Direct selling as an avenue of growth for women of color

"In direct selling the sky is the limit," says Alfreda Strong, District Sales Manager for JAFRA Cosmetics, International. "If you are the kind of person who has dreams and wants a better life for yourself and your family, direct selling is the place where no one can stop you. The only person who can really stop you is 'you' and the self-imposed limitations you place on your ability to succeed. This industry gives you all you need—and more—to live your life dreams."

The Direct Selling Association (DSA) (*www.dsa.org*) confirms that more and more persons of color—especially women—view direct selling as the fast track to personal success and wealth. And, while the majority of these individuals are Hispanic, there is much room for growth in attracting more Black, Asian, and women of other ethnic and cultural groups to experience the successes offered by this industry. More aggressive recruiting of African-American and Asian women as independent distributors and company employees is needed, along with stronger image reinforcement in web, catalog, and external advertising.

The Direct Selling Women's Alliance (DSWA) corroborates the power of women of color in the direct selling industry. According to its president, Nicki Keohohou, a Native American woman, almost 30 percent of its members who represent independent distributors from around the world, are women of color. A growing number of women are actively searching for tools to help increase their knowledge of the ethnic women's market and of how to effectively market and sell to them. Ms. Keohohou has launched Diversity DSWA (*www.dswa.org*) in response to the growing demand for insights about women of color. She says, "We have an incredible opportunity to support our women distributors with tools, information, and insights that will help them grow their business among diverse and multicultural audiences. The DSWA is committed to being a leader in this area."

We've come a long way . . . but still have a way to go

Despite the growth of women-of-color entrepreneurs, there are challenges. Specifically, the income disparity women experience in the corporate sector persists in the entrepreneurial sector as well. On average, women aged 15 and older who worked full time, year-round, in 2004 earned 77 cents for every one dollar their male counterparts earned. Among entrepreneurs, a similar phenomenon occurs. White women business owners generate only 27 cents for every dollar generated by their White male counterparts. Native American and Asian businesswomen owners fare slightly better: they generate 48 cents and 43 cents, respectively for every dollar generated by their male counterparts. Latina and Black women fare the worst among women of color, earning only 38 cents and 35 cents, respectively for every dollar generated by their male counterparts.

The picture grows bleaker yet when you compare average gross receipts of women of color to average gross receipts of White male business owners. In this scenario, ethnic women business owners generate a mere 14 cents for every dollar generated by a successful White male business owner.

▶ Figure 8.12   Average revenue per firm by gender and ethnicity, 2002

Business Owner	Average Revenue	Index vs. White Male Business Owners
White male business owners	$565,289	100
Women-of-color business owners	$76,877	14

Source: U.S. Bureau of Labor Statistics

Reasons for disparity in gross sales receipts

Several organizations, including the Center for Women's Business Research, have begun to explore reasons for the income disparity among women of color. According to their report, ". . . being a business owner who is a woman of color can evoke misperceptions about business capacity, result in lessened access to capital for business growth, create the challenge of balancing the expectations and demands of running a business and being part of a diverse culture, and increase the difficulty of attracting top talent." The research also pointed out that many women business owners of color have a double bottom line. They work to give back to their communities as well as for profits.

I interviewed several entrepreneurs for this book and found similar comments as to what may be holding back women of color from higher economic gains.

1. "Your net worth is driven by your network."

In the absence of large marketing and advertising budgets to build awareness of their businesses, entrepreneurs have to rely on word-of-mouth and face-to-face communication as the primary means of making their services known to prospective buyers. The Internet has certainly helped build awareness, but fundamentally, women need to feel comfortable in proactively selling their services to people they know and people they don't know. It requires getting outside of their comfort zones and meeting new people. Sometimes this can be a challenge for novice entrepreneurs. According to Therez Fleetwood, designer, author, and business owner of the Therez Fleetwood Bridal Design Company,

> "Our downfall is that we get stuck selling to 'our own people' and not diversifying into other markets . . . I think we lack expanding our networks and do not consider others who may want our products and services."

The familiar words, "it's not who you know, but who knows you" are important to entrepreneurs. Latina and Asian entrepreneurs, who, although more successful than African-American entrepreneurs in generating revenue, and who often come to this country as immigrants speaking a language other than English, have further challenges that make network expansion difficult. For these entrepreneurs, social capital or networks become very influential and create avenues of exponential growth as one network of associates is introduced to another. Both formal and informal organizations (churches, sororities, clubs, professional groups, families, hobbies, special interest groups, business networks, etc.)

play a key role in driving success for women-of-color entrepreneurs. It is also important to ensure that there is a good balance of both women only and male-female network affiliations. Each serves a vital role in building relationships with key stakeholders.

2. Limited capital resources

According to the Center for Women's Business Research, Asian Americans provide 24 percent of the total equity investments in their businesses, compared with 13 percent among Hispanics and 12 percent among African Americans. This higher rate of equity investment, or capital infusion, is suggested as one of the reasons Asian entrepreneurs—both male and female—generate higher gross sales receipts than any other ethnic group. A secondary assumption for the higher success rate of Asian firms is believed to be associated with the higher educational attainment of this group, which we've discussed in earlier chapters.

3. Lack of a business plan

Another major derailment to success is operating without a clear-cut plan and well-thought-out structure to support one's vision. Some women of color start businesses based on creative impulses without a clearly thought-out plan of action or a defined business structure. Many are the sole breadwinners in their families and they create businesses to raise extra cash to support their families. They need to have solid structure for their companies. Addressing these issues will help mitigate the challenges women-of-color entrepreneurs face in growing their business.

THINK ABOUT IT

Women of color are successfully breaking through and creating businesses at a record rate.

- Does your supplier base include businesses owned by women of color?

- How well are you tapping into the business services and products offered by highly capable and efficient women-of-color majority business owners?

- How can you provide important networking support to these women businesses?

- If your company is a direct seller, do you aggressively promote to women of color?

- What is your current plan to increase diversity of your independent distributor base to include women-of-color micro-entrepreneurs? Latina? Black? Asian?

PART FOUR
Sustaining Strategies for Growth

NINE

Corporate Commitment and Marketing Strategy

It starts with CEO commitment

In order for any woman-of-color marketing and sales strategy to be successful and have resounding, long-term impact, it is essential that the senior-most leadership of the organization demonstrate clear commitment to the program. It must be understood at all levels of the organization that marketing to women of color is a business imperative—one that is capable of driving both top line and bottom line sales results. Only the CEO and chief commander of a company can dispel the perception that diversity is a social program, or a temporary initiative. Only he or she can fully integrate women-of-color marketing into the day-to-day operations of the company and ensure that goals are set, measured on a regular basis, and that people are rewarded for results.

Some of the ways to create a mindset of corporate-wide women-of-color marketing and sales engagement are to:

- Integrate diversity up front in the business plan and annual shareholder report.

- Include the importance of women of color as a strategic imperative in senior-leadership key messages, speeches, and communication—both internal and external.

- Establish specific sales, share, and profitability targets for Latina, Black, and Asian women prospects.

- Drive accountability for women-of-color results and reward performance through incentives.

- Create an organizational structure that focuses on women and women of color as a distinct group or department, reporting to top management.

- Ensure there are Hispanic, African-American, and Asian women throughout the internal and external (distributor) workforce.

- Commit and deploy sufficient economic resources to achieve market share goals.

Establishing internal alignment

One of the tactics companies have used to create strategic alignment of diversity within the corporate culture is to host a structured workshop with cross-functional leaders to scope key issues, confront brutal facts, recommend solutions, motivate the organization to achieve stated goals, and develop an implementation timeline. Done correctly, these workshops will create a sense of urgency and speed in developing recommendations to integrate diversity—in this case, the Hispanic, African-American, and Asian women market opportunity—into critical strategic and operational aspects of the business.

You must engage the *right people* to participate in the workshop to achieve the result you desire, which is strategic alignment of diversity throughout your critical business operations. These people and their respective roles include:

The Sponsor: Person who assists in identifying the issues, driving the need for the workshop and is a key business leader in the organization.

The Champion: Person who plans the workshop, is committed to change and improvement, is accountable for implementation success, and tracks results.

The Participants: Cross-functional employee team who will develop recommendations and present to the champion and sponsor for approval.

Coaches: Trained employees or outside consultants who facilitate the workshops.

Subject Matter Experts: Outside consultants or internal employees who have specific knowledge on a central area of recommendation (e.g., advertising to Hispanic women, new product development for African-American women, market research expertise in gaining insights from Asian women, etc.).

Roadblock Buster: Senior level executive in organization who helps to remove barriers to implementing an approved recommendation.

Owner: Participant and employee who works with champion to take responsibility for action item. Action item generally falls within his or her functional responsibilities.

Once your team is selected, you as a member of the workshop will have an active role in:

- Selecting the specific issue that requires resolution and problem solving, i.e., create a scope of work for the team to address (establishing budget appropriation for diversity and women marketing, launching a new program to recruit Hispanic women, restaging your website to ensure on-culture and in-language communication to reach Asians, African Americans, and Latinas, etc.).

- Developing a concise workshop issue statement.

- Identifying people with knowledge of the issue and ability to make a recommendation/decision.

- Ensuring that a competitive assessment of performance on the issue in question has been performed.

- Determining workshop logistics and location (usually one full day is assigned to a workshop session).

Some of the questions you may want to explore as the issue is being defined are:

- What is the current state of diversity and marketing to women of color in your company? What previous efforts have taken place? What learnings are evident through past efforts?

- What are the potential metrics that would be used to determine measurable success indicators?

- How does the competition perform on a similar issue? What have been their results—both successes and failures?
- What are the expected deliverables? Specific goals?
- What economic resources and budgets are available to support the scope of work and its implementation? How will the program be funded?

Once the workshop is complete, you will want to ensure strong tactical follow through on the recommendations proposed. Some guidelines are:

- Set up a follow-up meeting and progress checkpoint with the team over a 30-, 60-, and 90-day review process.
- Hold drivers of program responsible for progress reports.
- Schedule bi-weekly updates with team to maintain sense of urgency and speed.
- Create tracking reports on specific initiatives to follow implementation status.
- Share updates with other members of management and functional leadership teams, as appropriate.

Organizational structure and alignment

Once you know where your company stands in benchmarking internal alignment, you can begin to create a new organizational structure that fully supports the development of a woman-of-color diversity business. Creating the right environment to put greater emphasis on the women's markets requires an effective balance on the various pulls on the business—from the need to support multiple brands, the regional geography of where business is concentrated, the role of marketing and sales—and its organizational realities. Some of the questions that should be considered are:

- Are there many brands that need cross coordination? If so, creating a dedicated women-of-color marketing team may be appropriate and efficient.

- Is this a highly decentralized organization? If so, the new diversity marketing and sales business unit may require that interactions be formalized with other groups.

- Is there any resistance to advancing gender and diversity marketing within the organization? If so, you may want to ensure a high degree of authority for the new marketing and sales function.

- Is this a highly sales-driven organization? If so, you will want to ensure that the diversity business unit is also co-located in the "field."

Companies typically structure their organization by brand or region. The structure can take many forms including integrating women of color into the brand-management structure, where responsibility for growth lies with the line function, being designed to have a gender and diversity-focused staff within the marketing division; having a gender/diversity focused staff that works alongside the brand and regional teams for organization-wide integration and collaboration; or creating a woman-of-color group with profit and loss responsibility that works side by side with brand/regional managers to grow the portfolio. There is no one "right" way to organize for diversity success. Companies need to assess which approach produces the results most compatible with their objectives. The key however, is not to rely on the existing organizational framework to drive success among women of color.

Given that there is no one "right" way to organize a structure for women-of-color diversity, the following chart represents a snapshot of some approaches used by consumer-packaged-goods corporations to advance diversity within their organizations. With modification, this can be used as a guide to integrate a women-of-color focus, as well.

Approach	Description	Examples	Pros	Cons
Classical	Diversity and women's marketing efforts conducted by non-specialists. Heavy reliance on women/multicultural agencies for insights. Brand managers and sales representatives do not separate efforts aimed at diversity or women's markets from the rest of the business.	Rely on overall marketing strategy, including budgets and research to ensure all opportunities are effectively pursued. Regional marketing managers in high-density ethnic regions conduct targeted programs. Strong agency reliance.	Puts responsibility with line function.	Women and diversity marketing gets lost in the priorities; caught in brand silos; brand managers may lack gender and diversity marketing expertise.
Diversity-focused staff in marketing division	Full-time women and diversity marketing resources are integrated into the main organization, with defined roles.	Sales organization has women/diversity-focused recruiting and training teams and a community-relations liaison. Marketing has specific people to coordinate with key targets and to manage women and multicultural agencies.	Provides organization with gender and diversity expertise and focus.	May get marginalized; difficult to influence the line function and drive significant change particularly in relation to budgets.
Diversity-focused staff assisting line managers	Separate group at corporate level is an active force and an advisory resource.	Corporate community relations departments develop specific initiatives and relationships with women's and multicultural organizations.	Provides entire organization with cross-functional expertise and an aerial view of opportunities to leverage assets.	May not be fully integrated into line efforts; potential to be marginalized on key financial issues.

Approach	Description	Examples	Pros	Cons
Diversity-focused staff assisting line managers *continued*		Works closely with brand teams to leverage effective, targeted promotions. Liaison for diversity agency.		
Diversity segment line organization	Dedicated team acts as "catalyst" to focus the organization on the women and diversity opportunity. Relies on market research and agency intelligence for development. Has budget and P&L responsibility.	Manages brand and sales function for ethnic markets. Prioritizes women-of-color groups and develops strategy. Integrates efforts with balance of organization and brand teams.	With P&L comes responsibility, focus, and resources. Ability to demonstrate "wins."	Requires total company support to drive results.

Knowing how to structure your company for greater diversity success will put you in a stronger position to drive continued leadership. These samples are provided as important thought-starters.

THINK ABOUT IT

Take ten minutes now to think about how you can better align your corporate culture and workforce dynamics to meet the woman of color.

CEO Commitment & Internal Alignment: Are we on track and seamlessly aligned across strategy, budget, product, workforce, and marketing to optimize the woman of color market?

Structure: What is the best way to structure my organization to focus on the woman of color market?

Woman-of-color marketing strategy

Once you have the commitment and structure in place you can begin to plan your marketing strategy. Marketing, in general, means publicizing your name, program, and service to your target audience and doing so in a way that creates brand equity. Its role is to:

- Identify a target market.
- Identify customer needs.
- Work within the framework of the firm's product-development structure to create products that will meet those needs.
- Develop an integrated marketing program resulting in profits through satisfied customers.

In marketing to women of color, the same questions must be addressed. Who is the ideal target market for your brand? What are the unique customer needs of this audience? Which strategies should be employed that best reflect the cultural values, beliefs, and norms of this audience? Once these questions are answered, you are able to integrate these findings into all aspects of the marketing plan—product, place, price, and promotion.

The woman-of-color target

No matter what the product or service being sold, the marketing process starts with identifying the target customer. There are several questions that companies must ask about the target to identify their best prospect for sales. The same is true for the woman-of-color market, particularly since factors such as acculturation, country of origin, and language preference can greatly impact your marketing plan. Fundamentally you want to study and comprehend the wide range of forces that influence the diverse woman's buying decisions. We've covered a great deal of information in earlier chapters of this book to provide a clear demographic and psychographic view of the women-of-color market. Refer back to these chapters as you focus your target, concentrating on:

Age	Geography
Occupation	Length of U.S. residency
Lifestyle	Country of origin
Values	Language preference
Acculturation	Income
Education	Marital Status

Generating women-of-color customer insights

Next, companies need to assess what women-of-color customers really want and are willing to pay for. To assess what these target customers really want you must use a combination of data and intuition. Primary research using qualitative (i.e., focus groups) and quantitative (i.e., surveys and statistical sampling) can be very expensive. Secondary research (sometimes called "off the shelf") is less expensive, but also less customized.

Primary and secondary data are tools to be used to reduce the uncertainty of risk. The author highly recommends that companies work with their internal diverse leadership teams and/or external subject-matter experts to use their judgment and observe what women of color actually do rather than just what they say. Behaviors are far more predictive of attitudes than are words. That is why ethnographic studies of women of color are powerful research tools.

Traditional marketing research tools are often inadequate in capturing and sampling diverse populations, many of whom have unique languages and cultural biases towards sharing information with people outside their known circle. Yet, corporations fall into the habit of relying solely on mass-market research techniques oriented to suburban markets to make decisions about ethnic consumers. Companies need to assess the types of measurement tools being used to gather information about the market opportunity. Executed poorly, these measurement tools will underestimate the consumer opportunity and slow progress even further.

Ask yourself these questions to gain meaningful insights about your women-of-color prospects:

- Am I defining my customers the way they think about themselves?
- Am I looking at life from their point of view?
- Am I thinking about ways to bring my products and services to them, rather then expecting them to come to me?

**PRINCIPLE #1   Put yourself in the shoes of your
Latina, Black or Asian customer**

You can put yourself in the Latina, Black, or Asian woman's shoes through effective market research. We'll identify some basic market research approaches in the following section of this chapter.

PRINCIPLE #2   Get the facts

There are myriad approaches that can be used to obtain relevant facts about the woman-of-color market.

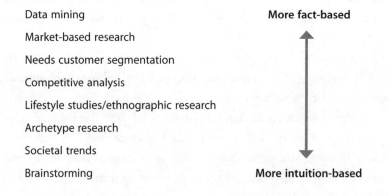

Data mining   **More fact-based**

Market-based research

Needs customer segmentation

Competitive analysis

Lifestyle studies/ethnographic research

Archetype research

Societal trends

Brainstorming   **More intuition-based**

The techniques range from being fact-based to intuition-based. The nature of your problem may drive you to look first at one end of the spectrum or the other. Toward the middle are lifestyle studies and ethnographic research—sometimes called "observational research." Within observational research, there is a similar spectrum of data-to-intuition based knowledge. This intuitive knowledge about women, for example, must be validated through the cultural lens of a woman's country of origin, language, traditions, education, income and values. Ethnography is a science based on observation where field researchers, guided by specific research questions and formal observation guides, actually produce data from their observational studies. This can be particularly effective in delving into deeper insights with women of color.

Data mining is an effective and cost efficient way to glean insights about women-of-color audiences using existing databases. The key is to be able to identify those women who are Black, Hispanic, or Asian and compare the analysis to mainstream women for major points of distinction. Data mining, or cross-tabulations, can be conducted from transaction data, customer lists, inventory systems, and other market research reports.

At the other end of the spectrum and using more intuitive approaches, brainstorming can be extremely effective in generating ideas about the woman-of-color target audience and the relevancy of your product or service. Some guidelines to consider and help guide the creative brainstorming process include the following:

- Use a woman facilitator from the same ethnic background as the target audience to manage the flow of ideas.

- Aim for lots of ideas.

- Aim for different kinds of ideas.

- Be flexible to new concepts.

- Don't judge.

- Write everything down.

- Be bold and open to new big ideas.

PRINCIPLE #3　Try more than one approach

If you're not sure you've found a strong insight about Latina, Black, or Asian women, try more than one approach. It's not necessary to always have rigorous analysis in order to generate insights. Get enough information to be 80 percent right quickly. Refinements to the approach can always be incorporated at a later point in time. Analyzing the competition is always an excellent way to determine what has merit from a woman-of-color target perspective, so be sure to track your key competitors.

Checklist of Brainstorming Techniques for Diverse and Women's Markets

Mind Dumpster	To clear the mind before a creative effort, take index cards and spend three minutes quickly jotting the ideas/ images/rumors/memories/sensations/emotions/pet ideas that you already have relating to this target audience and creative task.
Hitchhiking	Talk to commonsense people who are not involved in your task, explain your problem, and ask for spur of the moment thoughts or reactions.
To Market, To Market	Go some place where Latina, Blacks, and Asians tend to be and mine them for visual stimuli—stores, markets, museums, parks, construction sites. Bring an instant camera to capture ideas.
Newsstand	Use newspapers, magazines, radio and TV, and websites to find images, captions, trends that can spark new ideas. Remember to include Black, Spanish, and Asian language media.
Candid Comments	Use a video camera, tape recorder, or notebook and go to the "scene of the challenge" in the community. Record people, ask questions (if you speak the language), interview as many people as you can to get a sense of the attitudes, emotions, and motivations involved.
Magic Moments	Role play what happens from a woman of color's point of view surrounding your challenge, step by step, looking for the sensations/feelings/ thoughts that haven't been tapped by other brands.

Catalog City	Look at a randomly selected page from a catalog. Let what you see there stimulate new perspectives on your problem. If you were in the picture, how would you view the problem?
Do One Thing Great	List all the assets your idea has - big and small. Give each asset an award - Most Exciting, Most Traditional, etc. Look for the angle that you can best exploit.
Pin Pricks	Think about your competitors. What are their vulnerabilities? How can you best counter them? Consider sources of pride, endorsers, product changes, poaching customers, ways to outshine them, ways to learn from them.
Skybridging	On one side of a page, list where you are today, and on the other side, where you want to be. Fill in the steps to get from today to the ideal tomorrow.

PRINCIPLE #4   Test your hypothesis

It's essential that you validate the accuracy of your hypothesis around the woman-of-color customer insight by testing it. This can be done in a market research setting (qualitative or quantitative validation) or in market. You will be able to judge the power of the consumer insight and its relevancy in connecting your brand to the Hispanic, African-American, and Asian woman.

Assessing the marketing mix for women of color

Once your woman-of-color target audience has been defined and you understand this target from the Latina, Black, Hispanic vantage point (their needs, aspirations, cultural preferences) and how to best position your brand in a meaningful way, you can begin to develop strategies that leverage the marketing mix for sustained share impact.

Using the chart below as a guide, think about how your current marketing strategy is tailored to meet the needs of your newly defined women-of-color target market. Identify potential ways you can customize your strategy to be more aligned with this particular audience's needs.

Marketing Mix

Product	Place	Promotion	Price
• Product line range	• Physical distribution	• Advertising	• Price structure
• Design concept	• Supplies	• Sales catalog	• Payment items
• Color appeal	• Inventory	• Field sales force	• Costs
• Style	• Storage	• Telephone sales	
• Package	• Transportation	• Digital (web)	
• Brand name	• Warehousing	• Public relations	
• Service function	• Distribution channels	• Direct mail	
• Warranties	• Consultants, representatives	• Sales promotion	
	• Independent distributors	• Premiums and discounts	
	• Export	• Merchandising	
	• Import	• Research	

THINK ABOUT IT

Take ten minutes now to think about everything you've learned in this section: the target marketing, customer insights, and marketing integration. What steps will you need to consider before you execute your women-of-color plan?

Automotive Industry Spotlight: General Motors Corporation

Automotive industry trends, women, and diversity

Women and diverse audiences play an increasingly important role in the automotive industry as new sources of user volume. Between 2003 and 2005, new vehicle sales from Hispanic, African-American, and Asian buyers increased over 18.4 percent while sales among all other buyers declined 4.1 percent. Predictions are that by 2010, sales from women and diverse markets will grow to 67 percent of total industry retail sales from 60 percent in 2001.

In the midst of aggressive efforts to increase share of the U.S. automotive market, manufacturers have come to realize the influence women and diverse customers bring to the dealership in the purchase of new vehicles—both the positive and potentially negative influence their voices can have on purchase considerations. According to WOW Facts and Business Women's Network, a woman will tell 5.8 people about a new product or service she likes, but tell 8.1 people about a product or service she does *not* like.

Women are also critical in the area of automotive service. Specifically, women make 74 percent of all service decisions (where and when to have a vehicle serviced and repaired). In fact, women make over 39 million-service decisions annually. These facts make marketing and selling to women and women of color essential to the growth of the automotive industry.

Women of color new vehicle buyers

Women of color new vehicle buyers account for a disproportionate amount of all new sales among women buyers. According to Marc Bland, Manager, Analytical Solutions for R. L. Polk, sales made to Latina, Black, and Asian women accounted for approximately 25 percent of all vehicles sold to women in 2004, based on July 2004 calendar year-to-date sales, but 100 percent of all absolute unit sales growth for the time period 2003 to 2004. In 2005, women of color accounted for over 70 percent of the absolute unit sales growth among women, and nearly 50 percent of the absolute unit sales growth among women in 2006. And, despite a 3.2 percent decline in automotive sales among non-Hispanic White women in 2007 versus 2006, women of color continued to grow in segment sales during this time period, with volume up 3.7 percent.

Women of color are also growing at a rate 5 times faster than non-Hispanic White women in the purchase of new cars, trucks, and crossover vehicles. Sales of new vehicles increased 0.6 percent in 2005 (vs. 2004) among non-Hispanic White women; in 2004 vs. 2003, they increased 0.1 percent. However, among women of color, 2005 new vehicle sales increased 5.4 percent versus 2004; they grew 5.3 percent in 2004 versus 2003. These compelling facts underscore the vitally importantly role that Latina, Black, and Asian women play in the growth of the automotive industry. It's no wonder that maintaining their loyalty and positive brand consideration remain critical industry objectives.

According to R. L. Polk, average loyalty rates among African Americans (57 percent) tend to be higher than Caucasian new vehicle buyers (52 percent), with Hispanics (48 percent) and Asians (42 percent) slightly lower. African-American loyalty to GM brands is the highest among all manufacturers; among Hispanics, GM loyalty ranks second, and among Asians, GM loyalty ranks fourth.

Challenges

General Motors has represented the leading automotive company among women and diverse audiences for years, but experienced declines in

market share, consistent with other competitors and with overall industry softness. In relation to women of color, among the challenges the
company faced were:

- Preferences among women for small and mid-sized car segments.
  Women tend to over-index in purchase patterns for these segments
  relative to other new vehicle buyers. Opportunities are also present in the luxury segment to reach affluent and style-conscious
  women consumers.

- Challenges in the dealership selling and service experience. Extensive anecdotal information from buyers—regardless of manufac-
  turer—on dissatisfaction with the sales buying process. A lack of
  women and bi-lingual sales consultant employees, unwelcoming
  treatment in the sales process, and performance gaps in the overall
  dealership environment contribute to this dissatisfaction. Recognition that culturally, 82 percent of Hispanics prefer to purchase in
  "groups" versus 62 percent of Caucasian buyers have implications
  in the automotive buying process. More women and persons of
  different ethnic backgrounds have a preference to do business with
  individuals like themselves, prompting a need for more diversity
  and women recruiting in dealerships, according to CNW Market
  Research.

- Opportunities in advertising communication to balance main-
  stream/general market strategies with more targeted, on-culture,
  in-language advertising and using media that effectively reaches
  the audience at breakthrough exposure levels.

- *Perceived* gaps in quality, reliability, and durability (QRD), despite
  successful efforts to close *measured* performance on QRD.

Strategies

Starting at the top of the organization, with senior executive leadership
support of diversity as a strategic business imperative, General Motors
initiated a comprehensive and integrated plan to grow sales among
women and diverse automotive buyers. The key strategies employed

to drive positive sales results and generate diversity momentum were
built around:

Structure and corporate culture

- Create a sense of urgency for women and diverse customer growth
  by creating the Center of Expertise Diversity Growth Markets,
  a team of dedicated subject matter experts with budgets and
  accountability to drive market share among women and diverse
  audiences. Center of Expertise carried sanction of the senior-most
  leaders in organization and collaborated with divisions, regions,
  and corporate teams to drive total market share growth.

Measurement and tracking

- Develop an integrated business plan that starts with an understanding of women and diverse consumers and builds by working with the General Motors brand teams to ensure that brand
  development efforts are supported from a woman's and diversity
  perspective. Compliment this by working with the Field Regions,
  Corporate Relations, and Communications to have one integrated
  business plan that leverages all of GM's assets and speaks to the
  same consumer in a very synergistic way.

- Establish clear women and diversity market share goals, including
  "base" and "stretch" goals on a local, regional, key market, and
  divisional brand level.

- Track women and diversity market share results on a regular
  basis, and with key management and senior executive management teams. Provide tactical recommendations for share growth
  on a local market basis.

Upfront diversity integration

- Use tactical planning sessions to identify opportunities for diversity customer growth and "action plan" to eliminate potentially
  costly mistakes in not marketing to the target. For example,
  address opportunities to leverage common platforms, national

incentive promotions, and national organizational events to reach all potential customers, including women and diverse audiences. Auto Shows, corporate events, and national advertising all represent opportunities to reach traditional customers as well as high-potential women and diverse customers with "One GM Voice." Follow through, reaching all in-market "hand raisers"—persons who express an interest in considering a GM vehicle purchase in the future—through customer relationship management.

New product launch focus

- Design, engineer, and launch vehicles in major opportunity segments, e.g., small/mid-sized cars. The Pontiac G6, and Chevrolet Malibu are examples. Ensure integration of diversity in the launch plans for these vehicles with a clear national and local "go to market" strategic plan.

Advertising messages and spending

- Work with advertising agency experts in marketing to the women's market and to diverse consumers with targeted in-language/in-culture communications, both nationally and in key geographic markets of high ethnic density.

- Fine tune creative messaging with Hispanic acculturation/language segmentation, reaching English-dominant Hispanics and Spanish-dominant Hispanics with targeted messages on a local market basis. Use "on culture" Black creative to reach African Americans as well as crossover audiences (mainstream, Latino, Youth); rotate Black creative in mainstream media schedules.

- Use Black media for greater contextual relevance.

- Leverage communications that provide both a rational and emotional "big idea" to appeal to women.

- Go beyond the rational benefits—airbags, engine size, cargo space, and towing capacity—to include emotional cues that connect with women on a more human level. One of many examples of how GM created emotional capital with women was building a campaign around "safety"—a benefit that ranks uniquely high among women drivers, and using a competitive asset—OnStar—as the unique and differentiated proof point. Chevrolet in partnership with OnStar, worked to deliver this message in a safety advertorial campaign, "When It Comes to Safety, Chevy Surrounds You." The idea of 360-degree, all-encompassing safety is extremely reassuring to women in their roles as mothers, caretakers, and protectors.

- Create media spending and significant share-of-voice models for diversity, re-allocating existing mainstream budgets to provide greater allocation to the diverse markets. Incorporate greater use of digital/non-traditional media in spending mix to reach women and increasingly on-line diverse buyers. Because the cost of entry of non-traditional (web-based) media is not nearly as high as traditional media, and because women are strong users of digital, using branded content in conjunction with select target media as an effective strategy in reaching women and women of color. The lower cost of entry is very attractive. Magazines are still very important in the media mix. They do a good job of reaching consumers with their particular interests. Use premiere advertising broadcast properties to reach women and ethnic buyers.

Endorsements

- Leverage third-party endorsement of well-known celebrities to generate excitement, interest, and publicity among women and women of color.
- Launch the "Wildest Dreams" national publicity and promotional program with Oprah Winfrey. Over 200 Pontiac G6 vehicles were "given away" on television and millions of media impressions were generated overnight.

Customized experiential promotions

- Design promotions to reflect the lifestyle interests of women buyers and to encourage them to consider GM, while reinforcing the key selling features of GM vehicles. A good example was the

GMC Envoy Spa Gift Certificate program—a direct mailing that offered women a gift certificate for a spa treatment if they came into a dealership for a test drive. Previous information confirmed that test drives are among the most critical experiences a woman relies on to make a new vehicle decision. The GMC Envoy Spa Gift Certificate direct-mail piece was designed with an attractive, fragrant outer envelope to draw interest and reinforce the brand positioning of "unexpected comforts." The visuals, copy, and tone of the direct-mail piece were selected with a female audience in mind. One million units were mailed, approximately 6,850 test drives were taken, 1,700 GMC Division sales were recorded and more than 9,800 GM sales resulted from the women's direct-mail program.

Local market presence

- Although women are nationally represented, multicultural markets, particularly Hispanic and Asian audiences, tend to be located in parts of the country where GM traditionally has opportunities for growth (e.g., East and West coasts). Focus market share opportunities in these key markets, supporting Field Sales and dealer teams with local events, key influencer strategies, recruiting tactics, in-language/on-culture literature, on line tool kits, training, incentives, and so forth to help those in the front line markets grow diversity share.

Support dealer groups with sales training

- Launch the Women and Diversity Retail Training program, providing state-of-the-art training to dealerships and dealer teams on the business potential associated with diverse audiences, the geographic make up of the trading zones, and effective sales techniques in connecting with these audiences. Women and men shop differently; according to Envirosell. A woman will spend about twice as long as a man browsing the showroom floor. However, women have a higher new vehicle conversion rate than men do.

So dealers need to understand that women are not idle shoppers; they are serious buyers who have a higher purchase consideration rate than men do.

Studies also reveal a high level of dissatisfaction and angst among women as they consider the automotive sales buying process. Most women walk into a dealership armed with reams of research and files on pricing, model features, and options. They have a detailed list of questions to ask, which have been prepared ahead of time and checked with trustworthy colleagues. They select a particular dealership based on the availability of the brand and model desired, but also based on endorsements received from several friends and associates, both male and female. Women and diverse customers will use the Internet to investigate several dealership choices before making a decision to buy. And there are a growing number of digital sources to support prospective automotive shoppers (*KellyBlueBook.com, Edmunds.com, NADA.com, autos.msn.com, Askpatty.com, womencertified.com,* and more).

Through a research audit, GM sought to understand how women and ethnic audiences respond to the automotive buying process, and the impact of the layout, operations, and merchandising on shopping patterns of these audiences. Using a multi-faceted research approach that combined mapping programs to track and time movements and interactions of shoppers in dealerships, exit interviews, and mystery shopping, General Motors was able to assess areas of strength and opportunity with new vehicle buyers. The results were incorporated into a comprehensive, state-of-the-art training program for sales and service consultants on effective selling strategies for women and diverse audiences.

Increase diversity and women recruitment levels

- Recruit more Spanish-speaking sales consultants in key high-density Hispanic markets to address the Latino population.
- Compliment recruiting and training with educational tools for women prospects of all ethnic backgrounds.

- Give women control and empower them at point of sale, at the dealership, with Women in the Driver's Seat Guides. These were helpful educational tools with information on buying a car, service and safety. Sales consultants provided these guides to women along with their business cards upon entering or before leaving the dealership as a way to empower them with knowledge. In addition, the guides were strategically placed in doctor's offices, salons, and grocery stores. They were also used as part of a direct mailing and distributed at car clinics.

Results

GM stemmed market share erosion and retained its leadership position among women. Its share among affluent white-collar women (those earning more than $75,000 household income and college educated) increased. Its share among young women (under age 35) increased as well.

- Local market share in key ethnic markets grew year over year for three consecutive years as a result of GM's diversity integrated marketing and sales business plans.

- GM has at least one brand/model in the top fifteen automotive brands among new-vehicle buyers who are Hispanic, African-American, and Asian women.

- GM achieved strong word-of-mouth and consideration among women and women of color from third-party influential leaders and organizations.

- GM received several awards and recognition for diversity excellence.

ELEVEN

Beauty Products Spotlight: Avon Products, Inc.

AVON
the company for women

AVON – THE COMPANY FOR WOMEN, is a leading global beauty company, with over $10 billion in annual revenue. As the world's largest direct seller, Avon markets to women in more than 100 countries through over 5.4 million independent Avon Sales Representatives. Avon's product line includes beauty products, fashion jewelry and apparel, and features such brand names as *Avon Color, Anew, Skin-So-Soft, Advance Techniques, Avon Naturals* and *mark*. Avon's vision is to be the company that best understands and satisfies the product, service, and self-fulfillment needs of women globally. Its dedication to supporting women touches beauty, but also health, fitness, self-empowerment, and financial independence.

Beauty industry trends, women, and diversity

According to *Packaged Facts,* the beauty products industry of ethnic hair care, cosmetics, and skin care was estimated at over $1.5 billion in 2003. This excluded an additional $6 billion of mainstream products, which are consumed by women of color. Therefore, the total ethnic beauty industry is represented by $7.5 billion, a number that will grow to $11 billion by 2010 (Source: *Packaged Facts,* 2004). Against an industry estimated at $60 billion, women of color contribute a minimum of 12.5 percent of industry sales.

Effectively selling to women of color requires sensitivity to their beauty care needs and an understanding of the psychographics that motivate behavior. This is particularly true for Black women who have over 22 unique skin tones and skin care needs that distinguish them from other customers. According to an Essence WOW Study, 36 percent of Black women describe themselves as sophisticated (vs. 12 percent of Caucasian women), 34 percent of Black women describe themselves as sexy (vs. 9 percent of Caucasian women), 35 percent of Black women believe it is "extremely important" to have an individual style (vs. 15 percent of Caucasian women), and 65 percent of Black women believe it is "extremely important" to always look their best (vs. 32 percent of Caucasian women). Fundamentally, Black women are very aware of their African heritage, they take pride in making sure that they put their best foot forward, and they enjoy differentiating themselves from mainstream groups by creating an "individual" and "trendsetter" style.

Other noteworthy beauty behaviors include the following:

- 86 percent of Black women use a hand and body lotion product on a daily basis, compared with 66 percent of women overall.

- Dry, ashy skin, the result of dead surface skin cells, is a concern for Black women. Products that provide smooth, moisturized skin are important to this customer base.

- Hyper pigmentation, or the overproduction of melanin, can cause dark uneven spots on the skin of Black women. Women of color purchase products that provide smooth even skin tone.

- Melanin also slows the signs of anti-aging among women. Therefore, products, which are positioned as only anti-aging, will not have as broad appeal in the African-American market as they do in the general market.

- Black women will spend 30 percent more of their disposable income on personal care than women overall. For every dollar spent by a woman in personal care, Black women will spend $1.30.

Hispanic women are also an incredibly important consumer audience for the beauty products industry and for direct sellers. They are among the largest ethnic group of independent distributors, and growing, according to the Direct Selling Association (DSA). A report by *People en Español* (HOT Study) shows that Latinas use more beauty products than mainstream women and they over index on consumption. Hispanic women celebrate femininity at an earlier age. Latinas often have their ears pierced for earrings soon after birth, and are given jewelry (*un azabache*) at birth to ward off the evil eye. They celebrate their "coming out" or debut at age 15 (*Quinceñeara*) vs. age 16 (Sweet Sixteen) for non-Hispanics. These cultural rites of passage help drive higher consumption of beauty products among Latina women.

▶ Figure 11.1   Use of beauty products by Latina vs. mainstream women

Skincare	Index vs. general population	Fragrance	Index vs. general population
Eye cream	109	Use more than once a day	350
Face mask	187	Different scents for different occasions	227
Night cream	124		

Source: *People en Español*, Hispanic Opinion Tracker

Asian women also tend to over index on beauty products, but are more selective users of skin care products and skin care whiteners, in particular. Clinique's Derma White line consists of skincare and makeup products designed for use daily or only occasionally. The product mix consists of skin type–appropriate cleansers, lotions, and moisturizers as well as an essence, fast-drying mask, hand cream, and sun block, among others.

Challenges

Prior to the huge wave of Latino population growth, Avon had developed its most significant minority consumer franchise within the African-American market. The Avon earning opportunity, coupled with high quality products at an affordable price helped make Avon a leader among Black women. Historically, Black women held Avon in great esteem as a company that provided them with the means to elevate themselves in the community, to be treated as respectable businesswomen, and to become successful micro entrepreneurs. Few companies provided this much economic opportunity to Black women; this legacy resulted in a high degree of loyalty and respect among Black women, even to today.

Avon's strength in the African-American market began to erode in the early 1990s due to several challenges:

- Aggressive new competitive entries from mainstream brands attempting to reach Black women with targeted lines of color cosmetics (i.e., Maybelline *Shades of You,* Revlon *ColorStyle*).

- Greater numbers of increasingly well-educated Black women entering the managerial ranks of the traditional workforce. This reduced the numbers of Black women pursuing direct selling as their primary source of earnings.

- While Avon was perceived as a good quality company with a diversified product line, its shades were not seen as appropriate for darker-skin-toned women.

- Sporadic and inconsistent images of women of color in Avon's external advertising (television, print) and internal communication tools (Avon product brochure).

Strategies

Organizational integration

- Create synergy with field sales, marketing and segmentation through the formation of the Avon National African American Council (ANAAC), a cross-functional team of division managers, district managers, and marketing segmentation to develop business plans, identify new product opportunities, and create strategies for growth among women of color. ANAAC reported to the U.S. SVP of Marketing.

Product development

- Expand Avon's cosmetic product line to include deeper pigmented color cosmetics. Leverage Avon Tones of Beauty to deliver high pigment color, deeper shades, and rich color for women.

Leverage merchandising

- Make the Avon brochure more inviting and engaging to women-of-color customers through more prominent image placement of women with dark, medium, and fair skin tones.

- Use women with clearly defined Afro-centric features to provide authentic beauty credibility.

- Provide copy rotation of these images across Avon's portfolio, consistent with sales contribution for each category segment (i.e., cosmetics, skin care, fragrance, personal care, entertainment, gift and decorative, apparel/fashion).

Targeted communications and sales platforms

- Compliment the Avon brochure with a targeted, highly Afro-centric brochure, called the *Avon Boutique.* The Avon Boutique was designed to help promote Avon's image of beauty authority to women of color, to promote Avon products, and was also used to help recruit more African-American women to become sales representatives.

Sales recruiting

- Aggressively recruit Black women in key geographic markets of dense ethnic population to consider the Avon sales representative opportunity. Through a combined and multi-marketing strategy of local grass roots events, local radio, print and church promotions, Avon was able to increase penetration among women of color as sales representatives. This in turn, helped increase new customer sales among African-American women.

Sales training

- Support existing field sales and representatives—regardless of their ethnicity—in key ethnic markets with training, product information, and cultural awareness on the unique needs of women of color. It was important to raise the confidence level of Avon's current field and representative base to the business opportunity associated in reaching more women of color who represented disproportionate users of beauty products.

Advertising communications

- Maximize external advertising by targeting Black women with ethnic media.

- Integrate more Black female talent in advertising and complement this advertising with targeted print in *Essence, Ebony,* and *Jet* magazines.

Entrepreneurial engagement

- Partner with Black small business owners and designers in the creation of Avon beauty and beauty-related products. Feature and promote their products in the Avon Boutique. Corrine Simpson, designer of the Black Cameo line, was among the designers and entrepreneurs commissioned to work with Avon to develop jewelry with Afro-centric heritage to appeal to women. Products like these had tremendous appeal to the African-American market, but also crossed over to have appeal with women, overall.

Results

- Halted two-year sales decline in segment, achieving double-digit growth among African-American customers. Achieved a 14-point swing in sales growth for this audience.

- Created over 200 new products targeted to women of color—from cosmetics, to jewelry, to giftable items for home and family, to entertainment, to fashion and apparel. New products exceeded official sales estimates by 57 percent.

- Avon Boutique generated significant annual incremental sales and demonstrated an ability to sell to customers as well as to recruit new representatives. The Boutique product line also demonstrated an ability to cross over and appeal to not only ethnic consumers, but to Caucasian women who responded to the beauty and efficacy of the product lines.

- Closed representative gaps in key geographic markets through an aggressive outreach effort.

TWELVE

Financial Services Spotlight:

 Comerica Incorporated

COMERICA INCORPORATED is a longstanding financial services company with roots dating back to 1849. It is currently headquartered in Dallas, Texas. It is strategically aligned into three major business segments: The Business Bank, The Retail Bank, and Wealth and Institutional Management. Comerica recognizes the importance of women and diversity and it works hard to drive this commitment at all levels of the organization. According to Ralph Babb Jr., Chairman and Chief Executive Officer for Comerica, "Creating, retaining and managing diversity here at Comerica is a key business objective and makes good business sense. Reflecting the demographics of our markets enables us to serve our customers well, grow our business and build an even stronger organization."

This organizational strength is reflected in Comerica's Market Segmentation Initiative teams, which reach out to diverse markets including the African-American, Hispanic, Asian-Indian, Arab and Chaldean American, Asian/Pacific Islander, and women's markets. These internal groups, comprised of Comerica employees, are responsible for market outreach and relationship development. The work of the market segmentation groups allows the company to deliver creative, worthwhile solutions to the communities they serve.

In addition, Comerica has a strong supplier diversity program, which supports local and regional organizations. Some of these local and regional organizations include the Detroit Regional Chamber, Hispanic Chamber of Commerce, Inforum, National Association of Women Business Owners (NAWBO), Center for Empowerment and Economic Development (CEED), National Black MBA Association,

Southern California Regional Purchasing Council, the Urban Financial Services Coalition, and the National Minority Supplier Diversity Council and its regional councils (NMSDC), including the Dallas/Fort Worth Minority Business Development Council, Michigan Minority Business Development Council and the Northern California Supplier Development Council.

Financial industry trends, women and diversity

According to Eileen M. Ashley, Senior Vice President of Wealth and Institutional Management for Comerica Incorporated, "The women's market is about to explode! We see the shift in wealth because of the educational attainment and business ownership levels of women. Women are moving from covering their basic financial needs to acquiring real discretionary wealth."

Indeed, women, diverse customers, young women and women of color are increasingly important segments to the financial services industry. There are over 16 million affluent households in the U.S. mass market; 14 million of these households include a woman. There are 2.4 million super-affluent households—those earning over $200,000 per year. Approximately 14 percent of these "super-affluent" homes are diverse; that number will grow to 18 percent by the year 2010. Women of color, by virtue of their strong influence in family decision-making, will be at the helm of many of these super affluent homes. Retirement and financial wealth building services, college and education planning, vacation travel, home improvement, and real estate purchases are among the many affordable luxuries, products, and services appealing to this high-end audience. And young women are planning now for their financial futures. They understand the importance of asset allocation and why it's smart not to have all of their assets in one basket. They are savvy risk-takers who are investing for the long term.

Other trends to note in relation to the women's market and financial products:

- Women control 51 percent of the $14 trillion in privately held wealth in America. (Source: WOW Facts)

- 80 percent of women are in charge of handling their family finances on a day-to-day basis. (Source: WOW Facts)

- Women head more than 40 percent of households with assets of more than $600,000. (Source: WOW Facts)

- The IRS reported that in 1998, 2.5 million of the top wealth holders in the U.S. were women. These women had a combined net worth of almost $4.2 trillion.

Challenges

- Women outlive men by an average of 7 years and life expectancy keeps increasing.

- Women spend 20 years in retirement—five times longer than women in the 1930s.

- Women are concerned about retirement, yet less than half participate in retirement plans.

- Women are underinsured relative to men and relative to their (women's) income.

Strategies

Comerica Incorporated recognizes the huge opportunity represented by the women's market. However, it also understands that it has to step back and make sure it is not pursuing the women's market in the same way it approaches men. According to Janice Tessier, Manager of Diversity Initiatives at Comerica Incorporated, the company has taken measured steps to ensure the work it does to reach the women's market is strategically anchored against the growth opportunity of the market. I had the opportunity to speak with Janice about the history of Comerica's commitment to women.

"We've had a formalized women's initiative since the mid-1990s which at that time was called the Women's Business Enterprise Initiative. It targeted primarily small businesses and has evolved since then. Our strength has been in identifying different organizations to partner with, and in so doing we've identified NAWBO (National Association of Women Business Owners), Inforum, the Michigan Women's Business Council and CEED (Center for Empowerment and Economic Development), to name a few. We work to build relationships with these centers of influence. One of the major efforts we created was to develop a special product package for NAWBO members: Power Perks. Women business owners who open an account with Comerica receive a free membership to NAWBO along with a subscription to *Crain's Business Magazine,* among other benefits, as part of this Power Perks package.

"Comerica also sponsors many events with our strategic partners and hosts Power Breakfasts. During Comerica Power Breakfasts, we bring in a speaker who would be of interest to female entrepreneurs and invite members at no charge. This is done once or twice a year. In addition, we work with the Michigan Women's Business Council and CEED to build relationships with female entrepreneurs. Comerica also provides assistance to women business owners who are seeking to gain certification as a WBE (women business enterprise)."

Comerica has created seminars and events to better respond to what women want. The seminars were focused on physical and fiscal health, family financial planning, getting kids through college, helping aging parents, helping parents of special-needs children, and more. By asking women questions about their financial goals, Comerica has been able to put programs in place that are customized to women. It's not that women don't have the ability to understand financial products—although a simplification of language is always welcome—it's simply that women have to think about wealth differently. Women have a different set of motivators that impact their decision-making processes.

From the perspective of *The 85% Niche,* part of the success in effectively marketing to women and to women of color in the financial products industry is to understand that their motivations behind the attainment of financial security are different than those of men. Women may not have had the steady accumulation of assets that men have been able to generate because perhaps they've taken time off to have a child, or they've gone back to school, or they've not been in positions where there was sufficient income for them to set aside a portion for savings.

But with the educational attainment of women today, and the large numbers of women who are starting businesses and growing them successfully, they are now in the position to begin to put a financial plan in place that will result in true wealth attainment.

Comerica also took a holistic approach to growing the women's market by looking within at its workforce. Ms. Ashley reported that, "Comerica is strong in its support of women. How do you create that environment? It starts at the top. This has been something that our Chairman and Board have supported. Workforce diversity is a key element on the performance scorecard."

Increasing the workforce to reflect greater diversity not only has an impact on creating unique views but it also helps bring in new customers. States Ms. Ashley, "People see that Comerica has diversity at the highest management levels and they want to do business with us."

Results

Ms. Tessier reported results of their recent work with the women's market. "The 85% Niche was commissioned by Comerica to conduct research and internal benchmarking with Comerica management teams, field leaders, relationship managers, and clients. As a result of the research and findings from this consulting work, the Women's Initiative team at Comerica will be leading sales training on how to build relationships among women clients. This training will lead to increased effectiveness in communication to women and stronger customer service. The training will also help reenergize the sales staff with tools and approaches to reach the women's market. In addition, Comerica is expanding its scope to not only include small-business owners but also women who are affluent, middle-market business owners, professionals and retail clients, helping them with financial planning, business, wealth management and investing needs.

APPENDIX

The Boardroom Circle:
85% Niche Leadership Interviews

THE FOLLOWING are selected excerpts from discussions with industry experts and thought leaders.

Mr. Edward W. Bullock
Vice President, Diversity and Inclusion, L'ORÉAL

Mr. Bullock leads L'ORÉAL's initiatives as an organization that values diversity, not only with its products as a world leader, but also in its workforce, vendor and community relations. He is the recipient of numerous awards such as the NAACP and Urban League Service Award, and the American Association for Affirmative Action Corporate Award and Career Development Service Awards from both Rutgers University and Seton Hall University. He is the author of numerous articles featured in the *Wall Street Journal* and the *Black Collegian Magazine*. Mr. Bullock speaks extensively to organizations on best practices related to diversity on a U.S. and global scale and is past President of Young Scholars Institute, an inner city organization developed to aid disadvantaged youth.

> **Miriam Muléy:** You've held very significant and increasingly responsible positions with L'ORÉAL, Ed. What are some of the hallmarks of your experience with the company?
>
> **Ed Bullock:** I've spent 25 years with L'ORÉAL supporting manufacturing and human resources here in the U.S., in Puerto Rico, and of course, globally with our headquarters in Paris. L'ORÉAL distinguishes itself in many ways, meeting the beauty needs of men and women around

the world. We only do beauty—skin, make up, hair, lip, nail. You will not see us in an un-related industry that does not reinforce our beauty image. This is our model that has been successful for well over 100 years."

We have consistency of leadership as another distinct characteristic of L'ORÉAL. We have only had four to five CEOs in the last 100 years. It has propelled L'ORÉAL into the rare group of companies that have had 20 years of double-digit growth. It is a testament of the strength of our distribution channel, the diversity of our portfolio, not only meeting the beauty needs of women and men, but also anticipating those needs is a differentiating factor.

Muléy: That is incredible success, Ed. What are some of the best practices you can share with us in relation to diversity and L'ORÉAL?

Bullock: It starts with identifying ourselves around innovation and creativity, having diverse thinkers at every level within the company. You have to recruit these diverse thinkers who have that rich background and different interests. Also having a fundamental requirement, which is *respect* for the individual. That is the code of our business ethics. Our fundamental business is based on respect.

Our talent and recruitment model is also unique. It takes us into colleges and universities to identify the brightest diverse talent. We supplement that with various business games and contests. L'ORÉAL *Ingenius* is the premiere contest that allows undergraduate students interested in careers in engineering and supply chain to experience the profession through a real case study in a L'ORÉAL facility. The 2009 challenge is, "Sustainable development: What's at stake for L'ORÉAL's Operations?" We take those ideas and give the students feedback that enables them to be the very best they can be using an organized format that allows us to market our products."

Muléy: As you know, Catalyst has done extensive work and reporting on the positive impact that having a diverse workforce of women in key strategic and operational roles can have on return on equity. What does L'ORÉAL do to ensure that women are involved in the strategic and operational aspects of the business?

Bullock: I've seen that same report. When women make a large percentage of the leadership team you get a better return. They have a higher appreciation of the target audience and they are able to translate that understanding into logical business plans that result in sales. Over 62 percent of L'ORÉAL's total management is comprised of women and of our total workforce over 50 percent are women. Over two-thirds of our scientists are women, as well. So at a very fundamental level of the organization—where we create the product at the R&D level—we have a significant representation of women. Some might suggest that this is the reason L'ORÉAL is able to produce so many patents because of the diverse mixture of our teams.

The *Women of Science* program in conjunction with UNESCO is another signature program of L'ORÉAL. Through this program we are able to recognize the contribution of women in the field of science. We know there are very bright women who are scientists who seldom get recognized. So this is an opportunity for us to say to the world on a global scale that there are women's contributions in the field of science that must be recognized and must be appreciated. Our *Women in Science* fellowship program is our way of showing that women have knowledge and scientific genius in the area of medicine. This program has been in place for well over 10 years. It has traction, has grown in other countries, and is doing well for L'ORÉAL."

Muléy: I've had the pleasure to speak with Ms. Angela Guy, General Manager for SoftSheen-Carson. She spoke of SoftSheen-Carson's mission of transcending the needs and exceeding the expectations of people of color by "inspiring beauty" and providing premiere products for hair care and skin care. How exactly does L'ORÉAL view the women-of-color market—Latina, Black, and Asian women?

Bullock: If you look at our product mix, it's not by accident that we acquired the SoftSheen-Carson brands. With that model we have products that can address the needs of women of color around the world— products that are relevant to needs of African descended women—not just in the U.S. but globally. Our institute in Chicago, The SoftSheen-Carson Beauty Institute, is focused on and dedicated to the beauty needs of African-descended women. And we are proud of that Institute because it is a model of what a corporation can do to find the best formulation and best products for women of color.

We are not aware of any other company that has made the resource dedication and holds symposiums on a regular basis to share with other organizations, that addresses our skin, hair, scalp, the sun and climatic elements that affect us. The Institute is a rich reservoir of information that has not existed before and is solely for women of African descent.

Most recently, in 2005 L'ORÉAL opened a center at Pudong, near Shanghai, with the same objective—to study the hair and skin care needs of persons of Asian descent. L'ORÉAL not only has products, and has done research, but they have products that stay *ahead* of the needs of women . . . *anticipating* the needs.

Among Hispanics, we see great opportunity. L'ORÉAL has a presence in Brazil, and we have a presence throughout the world of the Hispanic market. The demographics for Hispanics are growing so fast and they over-index in hair care, skin care, and cosmetics usage. This market is a great opportunity for L'ORÉAL and one that we take seriously.

Muléy: Ed, what final advice can you give to marketers who are serious about increasing their market share among women and women of color?

Bullock: Knowledge is power. It is important to understand the extent of the potential that can be achieved by focusing on the consumer, but it is also important to bring in partners like you and *The 85% Niche* who can help you make the transition from where you are in understanding the market and segmentation, but also the strategy that can be uniquely formed to meet your organization needs. Partnering with organizations that can take you from a state of existence to where you can be is critical. Having that knowledge and then moving to having that respect for the individual, and the core competencies around cultural literacy are going to be critical for the future. The underlying desires to be innovative and creative are the twin sisters of diversity and inclusion.

Ms. Linda D. Forte

Senior Vice President, Business Affairs, Comerica Incorporated

Ms. Forte is a member of Comerica's Senior Leadership Team. She is responsible for defining and driving business strategies that establish Comerica as a leader in diversity and work-life practices. She also is responsible for the Comerica Charitable Foundation, Corporate Contributions and Civic Affairs.

> **Miriam Muléy:** You are a highly regarded and successful woman in business, Linda. What's part of your success toolbox?

> **Linda Forte:** For a woman of color . . . two observations . . . you can't presume that you are viewed without the attachment of race. We are very cognizant of race as opposed to a White woman who is cognizant of her gender. But there is no open recognition of that, for example, "I am a White woman" and then the woman part comes. For Black women we are much more cognizant of race first. We look through the filter first of ethnicity and then as a woman.

> I also trust my intuition as part of my toolbox. [Don't] ignore what is happening in your gut. We tend to discard the "softer" tools, but they actually are a strength and a tool that we should leverage. Sometimes when I mentor young women, I tell them not to ignore that tool. Often there is pressure to assimilate. But take into your repertoire—your tool box—your portfolio, all the learnings you can have. Don't forget that you have some additional tools. Don't ignore your intuition. Don't ignore the ability that you have to connect with situations on a spiritual basis.

> **Muléy:** What are your predictions for our young girls of color?

> **Forte:** . . . On the one hand I am proud of our young girls. I am concerned about the young men of color. [The girls] are more assertive; they are less held back by the barriers that I have had in my life. They can see a lot. They explore a bit more about what they want to do. Because of the educational mismatch [between young men and women of color], I worry about our young girls and whether or not they are over-anxious to please men. They open themselves up to treatment

and mental things that seem important at the time. However, that assertiveness [that distinguishes our young girls of color] can begin to leave them.

Ms. Glenda Gill
Executive Director, Rainbow PUSH

As Director for the Rainbow PUSH Coalition Automotive Bureau, Ms. Gill's responsibility has been the day-to-day bureau operations management and leading the effort to promote diversity and minority inclusion among the global automotive community. The bureau has focused on building strategic partnerships within the industry in an effort to promote, increase, and sustain diverse participation at every level. In 2008, Ms. Gill launched the first-ever *Automotive Women of Color: Refresh & Rejuvenate* spa event as a call to action for women-of-color leaders in the automotive industry to come together and discuss issues of importance to industry growth from a diversity and gender perspective. She also provided marketing leadership to the January 2009 Rainbow PUSH Wall Street Project: Women of Wealth Luncheon and Workshop Series.

Miriam Muléy: Glenda, you have an aerial view of what companies—especially those in the automotive industry—are doing to grow their presence among women of color. I've seen tremendous gains made by some and poor attempts by others. What in your opinion, do companies still not get about women of color?

Glenda Gill: Companies tend to use this broad stroke approach. The thing about women of color that I see is the self-identity and self-assuredness that we have about our body size. We are very confident, especially the younger women. They are self-assured. They come in all different shapes, sizes and colors. I don't see those inspiring real images of us delivered back to us as validation for women of color. The only company that I see grasping this is *Dove*, with its *Real Beauty* campaign.

Muléy: Can you tell me a little bit more about the psychographics of how women of color feel about their self image?

Gill: Women of color are not so hung up on, "I've got to be a certain size."

They really appreciate that they have full bodies. They appreciate their endowments and the endowments of their bodies in a way that other women—Caucasian women—do not. I think that they [companies] miss the boat by trying to speak to us with one broad stroke approach; we are very different. They don't get it and they *don't want* to get it. If they want to stay in business they need to get their act together.

They don't use us in focus groups in large numbers. We are not represented in research, and if we are in the research studies, they don't know how to speak to us.

We are also very outspoken people; we have our own opinion about the world and that needs to be heard. If they listened to us it would give them a better handle on that market place they are trying to grow. If you are not utilizing the traditional tools that are used in the general market—for product development, packaging, and advertising—then you miss the boat entirely.

Muléy: How does workforce diversity play into the equation for success in your opinion?

Gill: If there is no diversity in workforce, companies lose the connectivity with the market. They *don't have a grasp* of the marketplace. That is the first line of defense. If you don't have an internal staff then you are truly lost.

Ms. Deborah Gray-Young
Media & Communication Specialist

Ms. Deborah Gray-Young is a seasoned marketing communications professional with 25 years' experience in developing and implementing strategic marketing communications plans. As Director of Media Services at EMC, Ms. Gray-Young's responsibilities include managing the staff, budgets and deliverables of strategic traditional and digital media planning and buying functions for the agency's clients. Over the past three years she has directed the planning and stewardship of $150 million in client spending for Fortune 500 clients, including Wal-Mart, Tyson Foods, and American Family Insurance.

Miriam Muléy: What are some of the fundamental truths about women of color versus women in general in your opinion?

Deborah Gray-Young: Women of color *drive the prosperity* for our segment. More African-American women work . . . and that causes them to have more influence and purchase power than other groups. You see that played out in home purchasing, for example. There is also a wealth multiplier . . . appliances, cars, children's clothes, furniture, when you buy a house you need these accessories. We influence all of the auxiliary products.

Even if we don't make as much as White women, we still have greater command than women in general. Single women who will never be married are a number that will grow over time.

Muléy: Looking to the future and the dynamics in play from a social, cultural, and economic point of view with more women of color gaining access to education, entering management ranks, opening businesses, what are the implications for traditional Black family life?

Gray-Young: I'm not that optimistic about the [traditional] "wives and mothers" piece. You can't look at that [the growth of women of color] and not look at what is happening to the men. It is a very powerful downward spiral. I'm not sure what puts it [referring to men of color] back up on a positive course.

Muléy: Are people truly aware of what is happening from a family values perspective? What about our youth?

Gray-Young: A lot of folks are trying to snap people out of it—like Bill Cosby—getting people to break out of this stupor. Unfortunately it is starting to affect our young women. They have taken on all of the disparaging and negative imagery. It is starting to take over their consciousness now. [Referring to music] . . . where it started as great music to dance to, it has now infiltrated their consciousness and impacted their behavior.

Some of the things going on in school are beyond alarming. There are no words for what goes on in some of these schools. I just want to pass out when I hear some of the things these young girls are doing. Where does that go? Fast-forward 10 years from now, I don't know where that will go.

Muléy: Do you think we will be able to pass on the gains made by African-American women of today to our youth? To young girls of color?

Gray-Young: They won't be prepared. We may lose some of the ground. They are so preoccupied with other stuff, they will wake up late. The flip side of it is that I detect a subtext in relation to acceptance of diversity among youth. Yes, I am Black, you are White, Hispanic, Indian and that's all cool, but the tolerance is at a certain socio-economic level. There are still very segregated lower-income populations where you have isolated groups. The incomes prevent them from living in a diverse area.

Muléy: So, just because there is an increase of diverse representation among our youth, it does not automatically create an *acceptance* of diversity. People still need to be exposed to, mingle with, and be open to friendships, learning, and working with other groups of people who look, act, and speak differently from you. Young people of color who are isolated from those experiences won't be as open to acceptance as those who are.

Gray-Young: Yes. There are kids going into the regular public schools who are in trouble. They have no textbooks. They are not being taught . . . functionally illiterate, susceptible to gang violence, and more. The acceptance of diversity among our youth is greater at the higher economic level where you have less isolation from other groups and more exposure (through school, for example) to learn about other cultures and to actually sit in class with diverse groups.

Josy Laza Gallagher
Senior Consultant, FutureWork Institute, Inc.

Josy Laza Gallagher has over 25 years in the areas of Human Resources and Organizational Development. Ms. Gallagher has had a successful history in managing, recruiting/staffing, compensation, training, and organizational development, in the United States and overseas. She has strong communication, coaching and facilitation skills and a demonstrated track record of building relationships that support business objectives. She is Afro-Cuban, fluent in Spanish and French, has lived and worked in Paris, France and Geneva, Switzerland and enjoys and appreciates cultural diversity. Ms. Gallagher is a founding member of the Career Women's Forum in Geneva, Switzerland and is a founding member, Vice President and Program Chair of Madrinas, a virtual network for corporate Latinas, and is a member of the Organizational Development Organization and Society for Human Resources Management. She does volunteer work in the area of organizational development in Cuba.

Miriam Muléy: Being a Latina, how did that help or hinder you from a career perspective?

Josy Laza Gallagher: For the longest time, I could not separate my Blackness from my "Latinaness." People responded to me as a Black woman. I was seen as a Black person sitting at the decision-making table of Fortune 100 companies. I think when people saw me as a Cuban, it gave me a bit of an exotic nature. Whatever biases they had about Black women were overlooked. However, [the shift in perception] did not open doors [in corporate].

My parents always told me growing up to work hard, and study hard. I didn't realize the things being done to me [in a corporate environment]. My parents couldn't help me [in my career quest] because they didn't know about these things. Where there was more coaching was from Black friends.

I had to work three times harder because I was a woman and I was Black. They did not register that I was Latina. If I were more politically savvy, I could have gone up faster in the organization.

My husband, a *gringo*, . . . likes rice and beans. He is Irish American. We have been married almost 30 years and have four children.

Muléy: Hispanic women are doing double duty—excelling, not giving up on responsibilities with work, husbands, and children. What are the implications on work-life balance.

Laza Gallagher: I think that has always been a struggle (work-life balance). When you are at work, you are very American and at home I am very Latina. There is a shifting that takes place. You are nurturing, and you are there for your family, but at work you need to do more.

We [Latinas] have to do it 200 percent. For a Latina woman it [the culture] is more ingrained. We have to do it all and take care of everyone and handle the entire family.

My husband [an American] does laundry; he is very supportive. However, I traveled a lot, especially earlier in my career. My mother didn't approve. "*Tienes suerte que te casaste con un Americano porque un Latino no te hubiera dejado . . .*" ["You are lucky that you married an American, because a Latino would not have let you . . ."] Even in the young Latinos I see that attitude of non-conforming. My husband is very proud of what I am doing.

Muléy: What do companies still not understand about us?

Laza Gallagher: Our diversity within our [Latino] group is not known by American companies. We do share common values, but there is still that diversity. Family is still so important and I think we as Latinas have a sense of the work ethic and integrity that is unique. How we interact with family and friends is so different from other groups. My husband has become more relaxed over time . . . the hugs, the kisses [is different for Latinos]. I can see that they are uncomfortable at first in [our way of contact]. Being respectful, loving, and part of the family and extended family is also very important. I still send money to my family in Cuba.

Our traditions are dear to us. And from a workplace perspective we have a strong work ethic and a great deal of integrity. Companies need to know that about Latinas from an employee perspective. They don't get that about us. Even though family is important, they make the assumption that we will compromise work, but they don't realize that we are superwomen . . . we don't let anything down. We are very focused on our families, but we are going to get that report done, not going to put our parents in a nursing home, we are going to do it ourselves. Sometimes this impacts our health, but . . .

Muléy: As an Afro-Latina, Josy, what are your views and challenges?

Laza Gallagher: Being Afro Latina—some of the challenges are not being accepted. There is always a concern or push back. I am trying to use the word Black vs. African American to distinguish between cultures.

Another issue is that Latinas are often surprised that there is diversity among us ... that is more hurtful. Hispanics don't accept the diversity. Media dictates Hispanics are White. Marketers need to help communicate that I am Latina, but also know that I am an Afro-Cuban. It's sad that I continue to experience these micro inequities.

Ms. Dyan Lucero
Retired President U.S. Sales, JAFRA Cosmetics

Ms. Lucero recently retired after nearly forty years of dedicated service to JAFRA. JAFRA is a party plan company with a multilevel compensation plan. The company's goal is to improve women's lives—financially, professionally and personally—by offering high quality skin care products for women to sell. The direct selling format gives women the freedom and flexibility they need to earn financial independence on their own terms. Ms. Lucero has been a central leader in the realization of the company's goals and in its distinction as a company dedicated to the improvement of women's lives—globally.

   Miriam Muléy: The women's market—it's critical for JAFRA—is the heart of JAFRA. Can you share with me how the role of women has changed and heightened in importance to the company over time?

   Dyan Lucero: Thirty years ago women were working outside the home to supplement the income. Working was a way to have diverse focus with activities outside family life. The difference now is huge. Women feel more *empowered* today. Women feel they would like to *prove something* to themselves and others. They are searching and looking to *better* themselves. They are doing something they believe in; they are passionate and finding value. Motherhood is great, but there is more than that. They have so much more to give.

   Muléy: What was that light bulb, or "Aha!" moment as Oprah Winfrey likes to say, for women?

   Lucero: When the women's liberation movement came, the comparison— the switch—went off. Whether or not women agreed with the struggle, it awakened something in most women. The younger generation—they were children then. Now they, as young adults remember how driven we were as working mothers. I was passionate. My daughter saw that but she does not want to work that hard. She is not willing to live her life that way. I gave so much to my company. My daughter wants to make a difference, but is not willing to make the sacrifices that other women—older women—had to make.

Muléy: It's refreshing to see women in such large numbers in corporate and entrepreneurial setting. I can remember starting out in my career, where I was the first woman, the first Black person, and the first Latina joining a company. I'm sure you've had similar experiences.

Lucero: As I network more in the industry and community, I see that men learn as well from us; working on projects together, they learn from different points of view. The value that a diverse group makes is positive—whether it is gender or ethnicity. There is more value that diversity brings to the group. The group becomes more creative. You learn more because of the discussions; the more differences you can have in the team, you add more value to the process.

Muléy: I know that JAFRA is committed to women's health. Can you tell me about the Go Red campaign and JAFRA?

Lucero: The passion of the Red campaign is all about women in red. That's JAFRA's slogan: women in red. The American Heart Association came at the right time and came to us with the "Go Red" campaign. It was meant to be. We are all about women in red. We also know that heart disease is the #1 killer of women. We thought it was breast cancer. So we wanted to be behind the biggest cause. It's having heart, it's all about passion.

Muléy: Women of color represent a $7.5 billion beauty products industry. We know that Black, Hispanic, and Asian women over index on cosmetics, skin care, hair care and fragrance usage relative to women in general. What are JAFRA's strategies with women of color?

Lucero: JAFRA has been around for over 50 years and we have been working with the Latina market for 35 years or so. The unacculturated Hispanic is a strong consumer base for the company and now we have first generation Latinas from Mexico who are coming here because they want a better life for themselves and for their families. That's the whole reason they come. And they are willing to work as hard as they can to make that happen. "I will do whatever I need to do to make that a reality for my family." She has a work ethic that is extremely high and then you marry that with the beauty business and a great income opportunity. She loves makeup, she loves fragrance, it is inbred in her. JAFRA has been the vehicle to help Latinas reach their goal.

Muléy: That's a great business model. How does the company grow penetration among younger Latinas, who have more education, more choices, and more options than their mothers and grandmothers may have had? How do you make the earning opportunity relevant to her?

Lucero: New modern, second and third generation Latinas who may be Americanized are still great dreamers. The dreams are still there. The difference is what she is willing to do to make these dreams come true. They have choices and want to do it a certain way. But the dream is still very big. They still have the relatives in Mexico and the connection to family keeps the dream alive. [These younger women] will discriminate more in the kind of work they will do. JAFRA still fits in; we provide the freedom, a great financial return, and an ability to impact other people. Their work ethic is also strong. What we sell is a need every woman has.

Muléy: If you had a crystal ball and could see into the future, what will the future hold for women as employees and as consumers?

Lucero: I would say that more women will work from home. They will find ways to get themselves back into the home. Technology will enable that. Women will choose to work from their home base. As consumers, they will buy more from people they know, and trust, and sales will be more personalized in the future. Relationships in business will become important; it's not just about getting the job done, it's about relationship management; relationship selling. That will be big for the future. Women will have more choices in how they choose to spend their time, in their personal and business life. Women will be more aware of how to break out of the "golden handcuffs"—the chains that keep them from their true freedom and realization of their dreams.

Yesenia (Yesi) Morillo-Gual
Vice President, Financial Services Firm

Among many, Yesi's key responsibilities include the Request for Proposal review process. Critical to new business efforts, the process involves coordination and communication with various individuals internally and externally; serving as a liaison with all parties in problem resolution. Yesi serves as the division's Records Management Officer where she implements retention policies and coordination. She also manages the division's workflow coordinators, a structural support system for the division's financial analysts, created and implemented by Yesi. In addition to her various roles, Yesi is an active member of the division's Diversity Committee, currently serving on its Heritage and Marketing Task Forces as well as an active member of the firm Women's Network.

> **Miriam Muléy:** What differentiates women of color in a meaningful way from other women?

> **Yesi Morillo-Gual:** As Latinas, we are more ethical and more hushed about certain things. We feel guilty about doing something wrong, where others would say, "it's business." If I am in a room with other women executives and we are talking about someone, a Latina would not want to do or say anything to upset the chances of that person getting a great opportunity, whereas other women may in fact say things to jeopardize that. It varies on what the opportunity is and who the women are.

> As Latinas, we stick together. Our belief is that we are family. Whether we come from the same or different neighborhoods, different countries, or share differences in our culture, we are still family. Sometimes when you meet a stranger, you are on guard, but when they start speaking Spanish and you discover they are "familia" in the broadest cultural sense, you relax and open up.

> Latina women take care of Latina women. I would take care and be more attentive to a Latina and a Black woman than someone else. It's an unspoken and predestined bond and sometimes a sense that we need to look out for each other because we don't get that from, or as much as, others.

Muléy: When speaking of promotions and job security what differentiates us?

Morillo-Gual: Someone once told me, "You don't have to worry about anything because you are a number." They were suggesting that compliance is in action.

Muléy: What differentiates us from a motherhood perspective?

Morillo-Gual: I don't really distinguish myself as a Latina mother, just a mother. Being Latina however means wanting to be there more for your children and sometimes that hinders our opportunities because we would rather go home than stay in the office. Colleagues have sometimes suggested I hire a nanny so I can stay and work. To me a nanny is not the solution. It may be the economic and advancement solution for some women, but it is not the emotional solution for some women of color.

Muléy: What differentiates older Latina women vs. older women in general?

Morillo-Gual: My mother, aunt, and other relatives and friends, they live in their set ways, their culture is firm and they are sometimes blissful by ignorance. They have no inkling of the stock market, the corporate world, or even my world or the problems and troubles of the world beyond their corner. Our individual fears and issues are different. They don't understand my corporate life; I may not always understand their woes—we are stressed out for different reasons. Sometimes I feel like my issues are more important and theirs are irrelevant. Bottom line is that I live in two worlds where I have to understand what's happening in my professional environment, then leave my vice presidency hat behind and go deal with family issues. For Latina women, no matter the different motivators, boiling points or how tired we get of a situation, we always feel responsible for taking care of family and resolving issues, even if we think they're insignificant.

Muléy: What's important to know about recruiting and retaining Latinas?

Morillo-Gual: There is an assumption that Latinas are willing to wait until they are past a certain age to excel or that we simply don't want to advance and are just fine where we are. I often get the "you're just a kid," "you have so many years ahead of you," and all in good time" lines. There have been times where I felt like I was ready for more, but age, at least in someone else's perception, was a factor.

In summary, being Latina definitely makes us different—in perspective, passion and values but it should not make us less deserving. Gaining opportunities may seem harder, but our passion drives us through because we are "go-getters." Personally, I believe in working for what you want—there isn't an expectation on my part that someone else will make it happen for me, I need to be out there making it happen for myself because no one owes me anything.

Bea Y. Perdue
Executive Director, The Johnetta B. Cole Global Diversity and
Inclusion Institute at Bennett College

Ms. Perdue has extensive corporate background and experience in sales and marketing with Fortune 500 corporations. In her role with The JBC Institute, she also provides strategic and operational leadership to PowerGirls—a program focused on helping young girls of color acquire the necessary skills, knowledge and experience for effective leadership. Among the programming activities provided by PowerGirls are effective communication and interpersonal skills, teamwork, creativity, and conflict management. Additionally, the program addresses "soft skills" such as appearance, etiquette, and community service, which can have tremendous impact and influence on how others view your ability to grow within an organization.

> **Miriam Muléy:** The work you are doing with PowerGirls is to be commended. Your vision for the organization must have its roots in your personal foundational upbringing. Can you speak to me a bit about that? Where does the passion for PowerGirls come from?

> **Bea Perdue:** I was very fortunate. My parents were upwardly mobile; my grandmother and grandfather were those constants in our lives. They

made sure we knew what love was. Sometimes it was "tough love," but it was love nonetheless.

Muléy: What about our young girls, what's important?

Perdue: On a positive note, they are very inquisitive and wanting to know. They want to know more about young women around the world. One young lady said I want to know what girls are doing in little places; how much they have in common with these girls is a goal. Their community and scope spans the globe. They care about what is happening to girls in Ghana, Saudi Arabia, and China. They want to know: What movies do they watch? What books do they read?

[On the flip side] young girls of colors are oftentimes a lot more open to things. But the confidence . . . the lack of confidence seems to be expressed in sexuality. They look like adults (you see a teenager, the mannerisms are adult like) but the ultimate behavior is still immature. They have access to adult things at an early age. They don't know how to use them. They apply makeup like a 30-year-old. They don't have anyone to tell them that this is inappropriate. Too much eyeliner . . . too much makeup.

Muléy: How do you find girls relating to other girls of color?

Perdue: Girls in a research study we conducted decided to sit with their like friends. For young girls to find acceptance, that acceptance is more widely found among people like you. When you see the cheerleaders, the football teams, the status link breaks the ethnicity. Then it becomes a division of economic class. You can tell the kids who are well off and those who are not well off. They are accepting of each other, but the first tendency is to be with those most like you. PowerGirls was the unifier.

Muléy: At what point do you find that ethnicity takes precedence over gender?

Perdue: That question has been one that at middle management women of color seem to excel and then they get to higher level and gender trumps everything. There are more women of color in middle management, but fewer that get to the next level. As I watch the presidential race, I have thought being a woman is really important to me. I am proud to be an African-American woman. When I see another woman and she is doing something great, I am fully behind her. Then again, there are these situations where someone is always reminding you that as an African-American woman, your experiences are so different from your majority sisters, because they just don't know [what it means to be a Black woman]. I know there are times when I have made up in my mind, "there is a woman here and she will get my support." The differences when diversity trumps gender, in my opinion, are *situational*.

Is it more important for me to see a person of color versus for me to see another woman step forward? Am I always in my mind looking at qualifications—apples to apples—or have I been conditioned to say, it's a fruit salad. And, I can't separate out the differences.

Muléy: And what are the implications of this from a male and female person of color perspective?

Perdue: Education among Black women is on a huge rise. On the one hand, we say "It's about time," but on the other hand, you ask about your men. When you look at kids and how they are being socialized and how they are being taught and not being taught, you have a theory that women are less threatening than men. Women are going to get the access and opportunity because they are viewed as less threatening than Black men.

And in reference to our boys of color, is there some disproportionate number of kids of color who are being placed in remedial programs? Is it justified or unjustified? What about the kids who do not have parents who are able to advocate for them in schools and in placement tests for remediation? What happens to them?

What are the numbers in college doing for us? If there is only one slot at the top of an organization, 90 percent of the time that slot is going to a man. Look at Fortune 100 and Fortune 500 companies and look at the partners in law firms. Most are men. Some of this will take time, just having someone at the table to advocate about a person of color and perhaps say in their defense, "You mean she communicates differently from another person?" Just having someone at the table to ask questions will make all the difference.

Leading Voices IQ Checklist

▶ **Marketplace Assessment**

❏ Have you assessed competitive activities and their implications when doing this plan?

▶ **Who**

❏ Did you go beyond demographics in the development of your brand target(s)?

❏ Is the target large enough to be statistically stable for media analysis?

▶ **Where**

❏ Does your plan spend to business potential on a geographic basis?

❏ Have local/regional trends been examined?

❏ Have local plans been customized to reflect differences in media consumption on a market-by-market basis?

❏ Have you allowed adequate lead time so that local media can be purchased efficiently?

❏ Does the geographic spending strategy match product distribution?

▶ **When**

❏ Have you examined seasonality by region?

❏ Have you factored "media efficiency" and availability into your thinking about when to advertise?

▶ **How Much**

❏ Have you used all available tools to assess an appropriate budget level for your brand?

❏ Have you analyzed purchase funnel/image measures and factored learning into future plans?

❏ Are you spending to present/future business potential against Latinas, Black women, and Asian women if appropriate for your brand/market?

▶ **What—Media Mix**

❏ Have you done a good job of analyzing media consumption habits of your target?

❏ Have you considered the strengths and weaknesses of each medium in the process of developing a media mix?

❏ Do you have full rationale for every medium used as well as those not used in the plan?

❏ Have you looked beyond traditional day-part mixes before you decided on this one as
the best?

❏ Have you considered and incorporated if appropriate the Internet, events, direct mail and other non-traditional media forms in the brand's communication mix?

❏ Have you leveraged mainstream media to reach the target?

❏ Has a logical process been developed for the selection of TV programs/print titles? Has it been adhered to?

❏ Do you have a detailed rationale for each medium/action recommended in the plan?

❏ Did you put thought into the media tactics that will differentiate the brand in the marketplace?

▶ **Overall**

❏ Does the plan provide a good strategic fit with your marketing and advertising objectives?

❏ Does the plan fit the brand's creative?

❏ Is the plan logical? Do the parts make a cohesive whole?

❑ Does the plan reflect a balance of quantitative and qualitative elements?

❑ Does your media plan successfully complement other marketing activities?

❑ Did you take into consideration other brand's media activities when doing this plan?

❑ Does this plan differentiate the brand within the category?

❑ Is a testing element included? Has past learning been applied?

▶ **U.S. female population by age, 2007**

	Hispanic	Black	Asian/PI	Nat. American/ Alaska	Women of color
Female	21,980,731	21,286,017	8,291,405	2,292,162	53,850,315
Under 5 years	2,404,500	1,755,104	600,794	131,241	4,891,639
5 to 9 years	2,061,980	1,643,868	555,739	157,200	4,418,787
10 to 14 years	1,938,199	1,690,233	551,783	188,829	4,369,044
15 to 19 years	1,816,939	1,787,664	537,091	209,167	4,350,861
20 to 24 years	1,709,626	1,610,313	552,329	202,383	4,074,651
25 to 29 years	1,849,615	1,578,015	666,808	179,477	4,273,915
30 to 34 years	1,815,192	1,416,144	742,866	151,102	4,125,304
35 to 39 years	1,695,450	1,493,628	742,652	153,353	4,085,083
40 to 44 years	1,516,724	1,538,473	651,855	162,355	3,869,407
45 to 49 years	1,299,836	1,530,090	598,181	170,430	3,598,537
50 to 54 years	1,036,553	1,341,563	537,360	154,111	3,069,587
55 to 59 years	803,960	1,100,056	453,740	128,155	2,485,911
60 to 64 years	592,671	778,654	320,428	95,775	1,787,528
65 to 69 years	438,835	596,620	240,054	66,512	1,342,021
70 to 74 years	348,428	481,978	191,681	49,156	1,071,243
75 to 79 years	277,580	376,466	151,379	36,762	842,187
80 to 84 years	193,356	282,684	104,453	26,994	607,487
85 years and over	181,287	284,464	92,212	29,160	587,123
Under 18 years	7,532,461	6,187,684	2,032,106	603,763	16,356,014
Under 5 years	2,404,500	1,755,104	600,794	131,241	4,891,639
5 to 13 years	3,616,222	2,977,211	999,711	306,218	7,899,362
14 to 17 years	1,511,739	1,455,369	431,601	166,304	3,565,013
18 to 64 years	13,008,784	13,076,121	5,479,520	1,479,815	33,044,240
18 to 24 years	2,398,783	2,299,498	765,630	285,057	5,748,968
25 to 44 years	6,876,981	6,026,260	2,804,181	646,287	16,353,709
45 to 64 years	3,733,020	4,750,363	1,909,709	548,471	10,941,563
65 years and over	1,439,486	2,022,212	779,779	208,584	4,450,061
16 years and over	15,194,320	15,835,090	6,475,558	1,773,437	39,278,405
18 years and over	14,448,270	15,098,333	6,259,299	1,688,399	37,494,301
15 to 44 years	10,403,546	9,424,237	3,893,601	1,057,837	24,779,221
Median age (years)	27.8	32.0	34.6	32.5	31.2

Source: U.S. Census Bureau

Appendix Resources

▶ **Websites**

General	
American Institute for Managing Diversity	www.aimd.org
Business Diversity Statistics	www.diversitycentral.com/business/diversity_statistics.htm
Caribbean Cultural Center	www.cccadi.org
Countries & Their Culture	www.everyculture.com
DiversityInc.com	www.diversityinc.com
Diversityonline.com	www.diversityonline.com
Multicultural Marketing News	www.multicultural.com
Society for Human Resource Management	www.shrm.org/diversity
Health Care for Minority Women	www.ahcpr.gov/research/minority.htm

African American	
African American Women's History	http://womenshistory.about.com/od/africanamerican/
African American culture and issues	www.africana.com
Biographies of notable African American women	http://womenshistory.about.com/library/bio/blbio_list_afram.htm
The Hunter-Miller Group	www.huntermillergroup.com
What's Black About It?	www.whatsblackaboutit.com
National Society of Black Engineers	www.nsbe.org

Asian	
Asia Pacific Management Forum	www.apmforum.com/
Asian Women in Business	www.awib.org
Chinese Historic Society of America	www.chsa.org/
MI India—Bringing Communities Together	www.miindia.com
Organization of Chinese Americans (OCA)	www.ocanatl.org

Hispanic	
Hispanic Business Magazine	www.Hispanicbusiness.com
LatinaStyle.com	www.latinastyle.com
Madrinas	www.madrinas.org
National Society of Hispanics MBAs	www.nshmba.org

Mid-east/Southeast Asian	
Arab Community Center for Economic & Social Services (ACCESS)	www.accesscommunity.org
The Arab America Museum	www.theaanm.org

Native American Indian	
National American Indian	www.native-american-bus.org
The National Center for American Indian Enterprise Development	www.ncaied.org

Women	
Anne Doyle Strategies for Leaders	www.annedoylestrategies.com
AFL–CIO Facts About Working Women	www.aflcio.org/issues/jobseconomy/women
Asian Women in Business	www.awib.org
Catalyst	www.catalystwomen.org
Center for Women's Business Research	www.nfwbo.org
Just Ask a Woman	www.justaskawoman.com
M2Moms	www.m2moms.com
Marti Barletta Trendsight	www.trendsight.com
Medelia	www.medelia.com
MyPrimeTime—A Work-Life-Balance Homepage	www.myprimetime.com/work/life
The 85% Niche	www.85percentniche.com
Work & Family Issues Families and Work Institute	www.familiesandwork.org
US Labor Dept. Facts on Working Women – Black Women in the Labor Force	www.dol.gov/dol/audience/aud-women.htm
Women's Intercultural Exchange	www.wi-ce.org

▶ **Organizations**

- **American Indian Women on the Move,** PO Box 60436, Los Angeles, CA 90060 • (213) 974-7741

- **Black Women's Agenda,** c/o PSI Assoc., 1000 Vermont Ave. NW., Washington, DC 20005

- **Hispanic Women's Council,** c/o Cecilia Sandoval, 5803 East Beverley Blvd., Los Angeles CA 90022

- **Indigenous Women's Network,** 1519A East Franklin Ave., Minneapolis MN 55404 • (612) 872-1097

- **International Council of African Women,** PO Box 55076, Washington, DC 20011 • (301) 565-9313

- **Mexican American Women's National Association,** 1201 Sixteenth St. NW, Washington, DC 20036 (202) 822-7888

- **National Coalition of 100 Black Women,** 10 East 87th St., New York, NY 10018 • (212) 410-7510.

- **National Institute for Women of Color,** PO Box 50583, Washington, DC 20004 • (202) 828-0735.

- **Northwest Indian Women's Circle,** PO Box 8051, Tacoma, WA 98408 • (206) 458-7610.

- **Organization of Chinese American Women,** 1525 O St. NW, Washington, DC 20005 • (202) 328-3185

- **Organization of Pan Asian American Women,** P.O. Box 39128, Washington, DC 20016 (202) 659-9370.

- **Women of All Red Nations,** General Delivery, Porcupine, SD 57779, Contact: Lorelei Means

Index

About the Author

MIRIAM MULÉY maintains a vibrant entrepreneurial business as strategic marketing consultant, diversity expert, and business writer/speaker. She is CEO of The 85% Niche, a marketing consultancy firm dedicated to helping companies increase market share among women—a group that controls 85% or more of all purchase decisions. Her goal is to dispel the perception that women are a niche, monolithic audience. She does so through gender and diversity-savvy marketing strategies that connect brands with women of all ethnic, cultural, and socioeconomic backgrounds—Caucasian, Latina, Black, Asian, Middle Eastern, and more. Her clients have included: Coca Cola, Morgan Stanley, Comerica Bank, Avon Products, Ford Motor Company, Merck and others.

Ms. Muléy, Puerto Rican by ancestry, holds an M.B.A. in Marketing from Columbia University's Graduate School of Business and a B.A. in Psychology from Marymount Manhattan College. She has 25 years of executive marketing and sales experience in Fortune 100 companies. She was most recently Executive Director of the Women's and Diversity Markets at General Motors Corporation where she was responsible for marketing and selling to women, Hispanics, African Americans, Asians, Youth, and Gay and Lesbian markets. Earlier in her career she was EVP, Marketing at Carson Products, a division of L'Oréal, and General Manager at Avon Products, Inc. Her colleagues and clients have described her as, "an inspiring combination of smarts, savvy, and creative thinking." She presently lives in Michigan with her husband and children.